T0356554

GHOST IN THE
CRIMINAL JUSTICE
MACHINE

GHOST IN THE CRIMINAL JUSTICE MACHINE

Reform, White Supremacy, and an Abolitionist Future

EMILE SUOTONYE DeWEAVER

NEW YORK
LONDON

Requests for permission to reproduce selections from this book should be
made through our website: https://thenewpress.com/contact.

Published in the United States by The New Press, New York, 2025

Distributed by Two Rivers Distribution

Library of Congress Cataloging-in-Publication Data
Names: DeWeaver, Emile Suotonye, author.
Title: Ghost in the criminal justice machine : reform, white supremacy,
and an abolitionist future / Emile Suotonye DeWeaver.
Description: New York : The New Press, 2025. | Includes bibliographical references. |
Summary: "An activist, essayist, and organizer draws from his personal experience of
imprisonment to interrogate the premises of prison reform efforts"—Provided by publisher.
Identifiers: LCCN 2024051642 | ISBN 9781620977880 (hardcover) |
ISBN 9781620978931 (ebook)
Subjects: LCSH: Criminal justice, Administration of—United States. |
Prison reform—United States.
Classification: LCC HV9950 .D49 2025 | DDC 364.973—dc23/eng/20241223
LC record available at https://lccn.loc.gov/2024051642

The New Press publishes books that promote and enrich public discussion and understanding
of the issues vital to our democracy and to a more equitable world. These books are made
possible by the enthusiasm of our readers; the support of a committed group of donors, large
and small; the collaboration of our many partners in the independent media and the not-for-
profit sector; booksellers, who often hand-sell New Press books; librarians; and above all by
our authors.

www.thenewpress.com

Composition by Westchester Publishing Services and Design
This book was set in Adobe Garamond Pro

Printed in the United States of America

2 4 6 8 10 9 7 5 3 1

*I dedicate this book to my
father, who taught me how
to read before preschool, and
to my mother, who taught
me it's never too late to
choose the right course.*

Contents

Introduction   ix

1. Rehabilitation, the Near Enemy
   of Personal Transformation   1
2. Imagination Solutions   29
3. The Lie of Personal Accountability   51
4. A Fight to Build Power   73
5. Police Identity Behind the Blue Wall   105
6. A Vision of Abolition   139
7. How to Change Anything   171

Acknowledgments   189
Notes   193

Introduction

The political reeducation of Black people became the most important thing in my life after a conversation in prison with a friend. I'll call him Wes. Wes invited me into a conversation about a trans friend and activist—whom I'll call El—who regularly visited me. In prison, taboo attaches to gay, trans, and queer people. Association with them violates a particular code of ethics that allows a respected group of men to enjoy relative safety from assault or challenge. An example of how this code might play out: as long as you pay your debts, don't steal, don't talk to the police, regularly shower, keep your cell clean, wake up early, don't take your boots off during the day (i.e., you're combat ready), and don't associate with trans people, you'll be respected and not harmed. Wes worried about what my open violation of this code meant for my relative safety.

The entire time Wes was casually denigrating my trans friend, I couldn't stop imagining El standing there hearing him. I knew El would've been deeply hurt. I also knew that they would've left the prison with that hurt and still, the next day, put their already endangered body on the line to free Wes from prison. I struggled with how to disentangle the love at the root of his concern from the white supremacist principles

I identified at the root of his position. I'd dedicated my life to Black liberation through prison abolition, and I was talking to a militant Black man who not only cared about me but had his own long history of personal sacrifice for Black liberation.

In that moment, Wes and I didn't share an understanding of white supremacy or Black liberation. For me, white supremacy is a three-tiered phenomenon: a power structure built on top of a culture built on top of an ideology. The ideology dehumanizes certain populations and incentivizes stealing power from them to sustain and perpetuate the white power structure. The white power structure is a hierarchy of dominance wherein white men enjoy the top rung and Black people suffer the greatest degradations on the bottom. The culture normalizes this ideology, transmuting it from mere ideology to an erroneous common sense, or natural order, and the power structure enforces it with rewards and punishments through systems and institutions.

Cis-patriarchy is one such system.[1] To normalize white supremacy's power hierarchy, patriarchy requires a gender binary in family structures wherein men dominate women; relationships that support nonbinary genders undermine the so-called common sense of patriarchy and its norming process.[2] Enter transphobia, the ideology that dehumanizes gender nonconforming people as a way to take their power. The reasons vary depending on the person affected, but ultimately transphobia preserves the gender norms on which white supremacy depends. Transphobia is patriarchy is white supremacy, and opposition to these systems paves all roads to Black liberation. Wes's analysis of white supremacy is limited by his own personal pain. For him, white supremacy dehumanizes heteronormative people of color to steal their power. That's true, but it's only the most visible component in Wes's life. The normalization of white supremacist ideology remains invisible to him, and he mistakes patriarchy as a pillar of Black families. In this delusion, transphobia protects Black liberation, because in his mind trans culture undermines the centerpiece of any liberation strategy: strong families and communities. Standing on that prison yard, our hearts breaking for each other, we were simultaneously friends and nemeses.

I imagine his heart broke because he knew me as "solid," a term that embodies both Black virtue and a history of self-sacrifice to maintain that virtue. My association with a trans person represented for him a crack in that image; the crack indicated an eventual break, which meant another comrade in arms had fallen on the battlefield of Black liberation. My heart broke because this Black warrior didn't have a full enough picture of white supremacy to understand that his ideology made him a white supremacist. When I call another Black man a white supremacist, I say so knowing that I too have lived most of my life as an unwitting white supremacist. I say so relying on the distinction author and civil rights activist James Baldwin made between white people and whiteness. That is, white is not a skin color. It's "a metaphor for power, and that is simply a way of describing Chase Manhattan Bank."[3]

The same year that Wes and I talked, I'd found myself on a podcast shouting at friends who were Black leaders in my prison community. Homophobia, expressed in defense of personal values, divided the room.[4] We argued about whether *Moonlight* deserved its Best Picture Oscar award. A film by Black director Barry Jenkins, *Moonlight* tells the story of a Black, gay drug dealer and explores themes of masculinity and homophobia. People considered it groundbreaking for its depiction of intimacy between Black men who are more commonly stereotyped as unfeeling thugs. My friends on the podcast couldn't see themselves as agents of white supremacy. Like Wes, my friends thought they fought for the integrity of Black communities.

I spent the next two years thinking through how something as pervasive as white supremacy could be so poorly understood by the people most vested in ending it. The answer is white cultural hegemony. "Cultural hegemony" is a term coined by Italian Marxist Antonio Gramsci that describes how ruling classes control society.[5] Gramsci essentially argued that violent dominance can establish power, but it's not enough to maintain power. To sustain oppressive power structures, ruling classes need to establish cultural dominance. They must take control of culture-producing institutions. Through these institutions, they create ideologies wherein their values (for example, hetero-normativity) become "common sense" (for example, the idea that healthy families need patriarchs). Cultural hegemony has internalized in us white ideologies to make us the agents of our own oppression.[6] I'm convinced that at least three of these ideologies are patriarchy, homophobia, and transphobia.

These ideologies predate the concept of whiteness, but don't let the chronology fool you. White supremacy has a lineage, and its roots predate the invention of whiteness.[7] The direct ancestor of white supremacy is European supremacy, or colonialism, in the fifteenth century.[8] In her study of what she calls "Protestant Supremacy," historian Katharine Gerbner dates the advent of "whiteness" to the seventeenth century, which emerged in response to Protestant concerns among colonialists that the Christian status of their African slaves threatened the racialized order on which slave plantations relied.[9]

Before whiteness, the racial component that unified Europeans was Christianity,[10] which brings us to the next ancestor of white supremacy: Christian supremacy.[11] Christian supremacy designated the European Christian as the standard for the "full human" and cast all other identities as subjects of European domination. The ideology grew out of a theological and political project to replace Jewish people as the biblical God's chosen people.[12] Europeans appropriated the promise that the biblical God made to the patriarch of Israel, Abraham, interpreting this promise as a right to rule over Jews, Muslims, Africans, and Native Americans. In a similar way, the Israelites in ancient times interpreted the promise as the right to kill an entire nation-tribe, the Philistines, and Arab Muslims in the seventh century interpreted the promise as permission to enslave Africans and other "nonbelievers."[13]

I see a relationship between white supremacy, Christian supremacy, Arab supremacy, and Hebrew supremacy. They're essentially the same phenomenon, their apparent differences owing to adaptations to changing contexts. They're different points in a single evolutionary lineage, and this lineage lies at the root of white supremacy.

Consequently, I define white supremacy as a hierarchal power structure that evolved from an Abrahamic conception of patriarchy where power over life, justice, and wealth proceed from the top of the hierarchy, and ideas of obedience, instrumentality, and disposability attach to the bottom. White men occupy the highest position and relegate Black people to the bottom, and the power structure's mechanisms distribute power to maintain and strengthen the hierarchy and its underlying ideology.

White supremacy is a social, economic, and political order, but it's also a cultural order.[14] The latter is too often unaddressed or unseen in strategies to end it. Contemporary history bears this out: it hasn't even been fifty years since freedom fighters discovered that individualist approaches to racism can't solve a structural problem. Abolitionists have normalized that discovery in our strategies for change. That's a victory, but we're now called to normalize a new realization. I believe we will fail to end white supremacy if we rely only on structural strategies and analyses, because the structure is only the mechanism of enforcement, not the thing itself. Beneath the structure lies a culture; beneath the culture lies an ideology; and just as individualist solutions can't answer a structural problem, structural strategies won't solve cultural and ideological ones.

If we shatter the white power structure, we deny the white supremacists who descended from Europeans the power to operationalize their iteration of world dominance, but if we fail to dismantle the culture at the same time, other contenders remain to take up the legacy. This is why I find James Baldwin's metaphor of whiteness useful. The marker isn't skin color but a way of thinking about power—who should have it and how they should use it. It's also the culture that evolved from the belief in some men's moral right to subjugate people. I classify anyone who adopts that thinking or perpetuates that culture as a white supremacist because unwittingly or not, they consolidate white power.

This is how a Black activist can be a white supremacist. It's why I call rehabilitation in prison a white supremacist project—it normalizes false narratives such as personal account-ability that seek to justify racism. It's why I say Christians and the police are, unwitting or not, agents of white supremacy. These statements may feel too sweeping, but I argue that white supremacy, over millennia, has become sweeping.

This is a book about white supremacy, which means it's a book about power. This is also a book about my life, the story of a doctor's son who dropped out of junior high school in Oakland. By the age of eighteen, I was serving sixty-seven years to life for murder. By nineteen, I experienced an awakening and resolved to write my way out of prison. Twenty-one years later, I wrote my way out of prison. During the journey, I became a journalist, a leader in San Quentin State Prison's rehabilitation community, an activist who helped pass California legislation creating more rights for incarcerated people, a co-founder of the first Society of Professional Journalists chapter in a prison, the chair of perhaps the first nonprofit in California founded and run completely by incarcerated people, and a prison abolitionist. I survived white supremacy and took notes.

In this book, I share lessons I learned in rehabilitation pro-grams about two obstacles that get in the way of creating a new world: the "imagination problem" and the "near enemy." The imagination problem is the result of the millennia-long proj-ect of elite white men controlling what is possible for us to imagine by controlling what we see, say, learn, and experience. When we imagine something, we essentially engage in a mental simulation or representation of various elements drawn from our memory and perception. If groups in power can control those variables, they can control people's imaginations. And that doesn't just mean imposing certain limits. It also means manipulating the masses into believing they're changing the world when they're actually only building a moat around the oppressor's castle.

The "near enemy" prevents us from seeing that we're build-ing a moat for the oppressor. Buddhists introduced this con-cept as it pertains to emotional states. Every emotion has a far enemy—hate is the far enemy of love.[15] Near enemy emotions are more insidious because they resemble the emotions that we desire to have, but they only undermine our goal. Pity is the near enemy of compassion, and sympathy is the near enemy of empathy. Compassion, for example, brings people closer together because it grows from understanding and identifica-tion. When I feel compassion for a houseless person, I know that there but for the grace of God go I. Pity separates people by placing the pitied person beneath the so-called benevolent observer. If I pity a houseless person, I think less of him; I'm disgusted at the thought of ever being him—which means I'm disgusted at him. We push away what disgusts us. The actions of someone who feels compassion for a houseless person, then, may resemble the actions of someone who pities a houseless person. Both may give the houseless person five dollars, but one validates the houseless person's shared humanity; the other denies it. I've translated this idea into the sphere of social transformation. Cancel culture is a near enemy of accountability; identity politics is the near enemy of centering impacted people; rehabilitation, the near enemy of personal transformation.

In this book, I share the story of how I wrote my way out of prison. I tell the story of how I co-founded Prison Renaissance—an abolitionist model of change to challenge the rehabilitation model—and encountered my most dangerous opponents in the people working for change within the prison system. I share how people misinterpret my success story as a triumph of personal accountability and why that interpretation strengthens white supremacy. I pull back the curtain on law enforcement narratives to reveal the true identity of police forces as state-sanctioned terrorist organizations. I describe what police and prison abolition can look like in a world where humanity has triumphed over white power, and finally, I share my story of learning how to change anything.

I wrote this book for people who want to end white supremacy. I pray that readers reach the final page with a deeper clarity about how white supremacists build and consolidate power, and how we who resist can build power outside oppressive structures to create a liberated world.

1

Rehabilitation, the Near Enemy of Personal Transformation

A friend invited me to dinner because she wanted to discuss Governor Gavin Newsom's prison reform policy. My friend's an abolitionist, but she admits she can't imagine how to abolish prisons and respond to crime in a way that society will support. Consequently, I consider her strategies as favoring incremental change, the reforms that she feels we can enact now in the hope they eventually lead to abolition.

The waiter seated us, and my friend described Newsom's reform. He wanted to tear down death row, build a state-of-the-art rehabilitation center, repeat this process across California, and then call the prison problem fixed. The project would cost $20 billion over twenty-five years, a waste of money, because a lack of shiny buildings isn't the problem with prisons. Not only was it a waste of money, but the money would also make the California Department of Corrections and Rehabilitation (CDCR) more powerful. I rankled at the idea because the last thing an abolitionist wants is a bigger correctional budget. The Department of Corrections invariably use their budgets, through their unions, to influence legislation.[1]

I told my friend that the reform didn't even approach being a good idea.

"But isn't it good that the governor's tearing down death row?" she asked.

"You want to save six hundred people on death row by throwing the hundreds of thousands of people this more powerful prison system will incarcerate under the bus?"

She didn't. She also didn't believe anyone could stop the governor's plan, so she wanted to consider how playing along could salvage some good from the catastrophe. Like many abolitionists, she contended with the practical realities of organizing against vast power structures determined to remain entrenched. She was playing the game of trade-offs. I wanted her to know that I understand some situations call for trade-offs, but we can't make tradeoffs that take us two steps forward but four steps back. I also wanted her to believe that we will never build a post-prison world unless we stop organizing for what we think people will give us and organize for what we want. But, as she pointed out, I'm just one opinion.

"There's a lot of support for this plan among formerly incarcerated people," she said. She referred to the advisory council the governor had assembled to co-sign his project. Several of the members were formerly incarcerated people working in the criminal justice reform sector. They'd once served life sentences just as I had. They had powerful stories of personal transformation and community service. Some of them had also received executive clemency from a governor of

California just as I had. So why not listen to all of them instead of the one me?

"You don't have to listen to me." (I didn't say this, but I'm saying it here.) "But abolitionists can't follow the lead of the incarcerated people on the governor's council because the governor chose white supremacists, and white supremacists are vested in preserving prisons' power." I know this because I know most of the formerly incarcerated people he chose. They're white supremacists whether or not they recognize it, and their ambitions for social change are all the more insidious as formerly incarcerated people who likely don't know they're white supremacists.

I know this because, like them, I had to become a white supremacist to get out of prison. My governor would never have commuted the life sentence of a person who challenged the social narratives and strategies of corrections. I had to act out a script in which I alone held responsibility for my incarceration, and not only did I deserve my punishment, but my punishment largely defined justice. I had to appear to be grateful for rehabilitation, the path laid out by prison officials for my redemption. These narratives legitimize the lie that prison officials are good-faith agents performing a public good. The parole board would never have released me if I openly disrupted the political and social power structures on which parole commissioners' authority rests. The parole board, in fact, requires incarcerated people to "admit" that the legal system that imprisons them is fair. More than that, the retired police officers and prosecutors who comprise the parole board require the incarcerated people at their mercy to believe that the system is fair, and their bullshit detectors preclude most performances.

In California, between 2010 and 2022 the average rate of parole grants was 16 percent.[2] Many people mistake this low parole rate as evidence that 84 percent of the people in prison remain incarcerated for public safety purposes. Actually, they remain in prison because they can't convince a parole board that they believe that the U.S. criminal legal system is fair. Because it isn't. The power structures of law enforcement, courts, and corrections are racist. They incarcerate Black Americans at five times the rate as white Americans.[3] Prosecutors sentence people of color to longer sentences than white people in similar situations,[4] and, although the CDCR doesn't collect or publish data on race's impact on parole decisions, the little data that is available affirms the lived experience of Black people facing parole boards: race influences parole decisions.[5]

Race influences parole decisions in ways that prove difficult to challenge, because states invest parole commissioners with deep discretion and little accountability. That level of discretion helps racism thrive in all spheres of criminal justice, from police officers to prosecutors to judges.[6] Parole commissioners in

California use discretion to weigh a number of considerations that determine parole suitability. Most of these criteria are static conditions such as the nature of the crime, family history, and criminal history.[7] A person who grew up in a single-parent home and was in prison for murder can never change these facts about themselves. Legally, a commissioner can't deny parole to a parole candidate for a history they can't change, but the courts have ruled that if commissioners don't feel that the candidate is remorseful enough or insightful enough or of the correct "demeanor," that is enough to use the candidate's history as grounds for parole denial.[8]

Demeanor. I've participated in enough conversations about how to prepare for the parole board to see what demeanor means in practice. In one conversation, a seventy-year-old man from Louisiana spoke about his continuous parole denials. He'd taken all the rehabilitation classes, he avoided rules violation reports, he'd taken college courses, and he'd completed every task the board had assigned him to demonstrate his parole suitability. They continued to deny him, and the only explanation that he or I or anyone in the room could come up with was that he had a thick Southern accent—that is, he read in neoliberal California as having an unacceptable "demeanor." This man's eyes welled with frustration as he told his story.

Parole preparation is an unpaid industry in San Quentin State Prison, and the room was full of veterans of the process.

Nobody could offer this man advice because everyone understood that success at a hearing depended on your ability to articulate your remorse and insight in a language and with a "demeanor" that translated well to predominantly white commissioners. You had to learn a language that validated their racist, classist preconceptions of the world.

The validation of parole commissioners' preconceptions also means the perpetuation of white supremacist culture. The pathway out of prison, then, is to dedicate your life, through prison programs and redemption narratives, to validating and perpetuating white supremacy. I did this. I attended victim's awareness classes to learn about the impact of my crimes on my victims and how to make amends. What I learned was self-abnegation. To honor my victims, I built an altar and sacrificed my truths. The racist criminal legal system that had been stalking me since I was boy watching through the car windshield as police frisked my father; the school-to-prison pipeline I'd been swimming against since the moment my junior high school called the police to discipline me; the conditions of poverty and violence intentionally created in my community by the Nixons, Reagans, and Clintons of the world—these truths didn't matter. Talking about them meant I had no remorse. The only thing that could matter to me was my victims and how I, an offender, would redeem myself by transforming my life into a daily exercise of making amends. Everything I did, from writing to donating my prison slave wage to charity, was an act of devotion to the man I had murdered and his family. Once I was on my path to redemption, the logics of this victim-offender dynamic were artfully expanded. First, I was helped to see how my victims weren't just the man I killed and his family. My community was also my victim. As servants of the community, then, the judges and district attorneys were my victims. Prison guards were my victims. By the time I finished sacrificing my truths, the cops that had been kicking me unconscious since I was fourteen years old were my victims.

We often think of rehabilitation as something separate from the problem of mass incarceration. It's not; it's in fact the institutional practice that goes the farthest toward legitimating the existence of prisons. We see clear, commonsense arguments against solitary confinement, slave labor, and overcrowding. Who would argue against offering incarcerated people free college courses, job training, drug addiction counseling, anger management and nonviolent communication courses? It's true that many incarcerated people need these services. What this truth obscures, however, are the white supremacist processes using the cover of these programs to "prepare incarcerated people to succeed in society."

What does "succeed in society" mean in a racist society? When someone says rehabilitation teaches incarcerated people how to navigate society more successfully, what I hear is that rehabilitation will teach incarcerated people how to navigate a white supremacist society on the latter's terms. Navigating white supremacy is very different from challenging it. The former is a well-established road to personal success in America, but if everyone chooses this road, it ensures the continuance of white supremacy. When I hear that rehabilitation helps incarcerated people reintegrate into society, I recognize that in practice this translates into conditioning incarcerated people to perpetuate white supremacy. The process is hidden behind the near enemy of positive personal transformation: rehabilitation.

Rehabilitation looks like personal transformation. Programs seem to empower incarcerated people to improve their characters, change their lives. What I think rehabilitation actually aims to do is spiritually and mentally annihilate people so that the state can rebuild them as automatons who become advocates for a white supremacist system.

Nowhere did this play out with more complexity and on such scale than during the three years I worked as an incarcerated journalist for the *San Quentin News*. *San Quentin News* is a prison newspaper operated by incarcerated people trained by volunteer journalists. In my time there, we distributed over twenty thousand newspapers a month and raised over $200,000 in revenue (none of which went to incarcerated people). We wrote ostensibly objective articles for which we received journalistic awards, but we were not objective. We only published stories about rehabilitation. Although many of us were activists organizing to change public policy to empower incarcerated people, what we became was the California Department of Corrections and Rehabilitation's most effective communications campaign for rehabilitation.

An article published by one of my mentors exemplifies how we legitimized rehabilitation each month. Headlined "Criminals and Gangmembers Anonymous Graduation," the article covered the popular rehabilitative group of the same name.[9] This group has adapted the twelve steps of Alcoholics Anonymous and applied them to crime. In Criminals and Gangmembers Anonymous (CGA), crime is an individual sickness, an addiction, and the proselytizing message of the graduates generally goes something like, *I was sick, and now I'm healed; you are sick, and you can be healed!*

"The crime starts in your mindset," one of the graduates, Corey Willis, is quoted saying. He's pictured in the article in downtown San Francisco, shortly after paroling. He's smiling, hanging from a trolley car, wearing a suit. In that picture, he's who every person locked in a cell wants to be. In his explanation of a criminal mindset, Corey said that he had told himself what he needed to hear to feel good about his actions. I know Corey because he was my facilitator when I was in CGA, where he expounded on these very words many times.

What he's saying is that he'd hurt people regularly because he fed himself narratives like, "I'm protecting my loved ones" and "I'm a soldier."

It's true both that Corey should feel remorseful for harming people and that he fed himself narratives to avoid feeling responsible. Rehabilitation culture would have the analysis end there, but when I dig beneath Corey's personal responsibility, I see how CGA's core principle—that crime starts in your mindset—is a misdirection. People in rehabilitation culture blame Corey for his wrongs and applaud him for his return to productive citizenship, but they ignore that society incarcerates people less because of what they do and more because of who they are.

If I steal toilet paper from a convenience store, I'm a thief who deserves incarceration, but when Donald Trump and his university steal $25 million from students, he's merely someone who has to return the money he stole. On January 6, 2021, Trump incited an insurgency at the Capitol building that resulted in multiple deaths. If I incited an insurgency at the Capitol, I'd likely be shot to death on the street without a trial.

In these comparisons, there's no moral difference that justifies criminalizing me but not Trump. Yet criminal justice narratives have manufactured a moral difference. Such fabricated differences often rest on narratives about how the actions of a criminal harm people or society. But if we compare the scale of harm done to society by just Trump to the harm done by me, Corey, and every graduate of CGA combined, it's clear to me that crime is not in any practical sense a function of the harm a person causes. It is instead a function of privilege. From this, it follows that we punish people in the U.S. not because of what they have done but because of their social position relative to the white power structure. A strategy for positive change that ignores this at best lacks the clarity to be effective. In the case of rehabilitation, it produces a near enemy.

It took me a while to see this because I believed in rehabilitation. Like many people experiencing a delusion of merciful salvation, I felt morally bound to pay it forward. I leveraged my gift as a communicator to convince other incarcerated people that rehabilitation was the truth and the light. Governor Jerry Brown awarded me a commutation for the ferocity of my efforts. People may have enough compassion to understand why I did it. But to end white supremacy—a necessary step in achieving abolition—it's vital to also understand that I was practicing white supremacy, and that the differences between practicing white supremacy and being a white supremacist are not of practical relevance. I joined lockstep with the system that oppressed me in exchange for the privilege of release. Again, we're back to tradeoffs. Do I perpetuate a corrupt system to get out of prison? Does my friend who invited me to dinner support a reform that tears down death row but expands prisons' footprints? White supremacy has survived a global revolt against colonialism, a slave abolition movement, the civil rights movement, the anti-apartheid movement, and the Movement for Black Lives because freedom fighters make the wrong tradeoffs every day.

My father worked hard for the American dream. He was born poor to a single mother in Baltimore, Maryland, where in 1949 white people were both weaponizing race to secure more factory jobs and moving to the suburbs to avoid sending their kids to school with Black children. The most viable path out of poverty at the time was higher education, and my grandma-ma worked hard to open doors for my dad. She spent her days on her hands and knees scrubbing the floors in homes of white Seventh-day Adventists. This was her pathway to getting my father into a Seventh-day Adventist private school, where he learned to hate his skin, worship a bearded white God, and submit to white ideas about what his skin meant—that he had to prove he was good enough, that he had to look past the indignities white people forced on him and be grateful for the opportunities they selected for him.

He earned a scholarship to college, eventually relocated to San Francisco to attend medical school, and became a Black doctor deeply scarred by white supremacy. That experience splintered him into a dozen people who, to me, seemed to be both drowning and fighting for one last expression before the waves closed in. He was a Black man enraged at America's lies about justice and equality, a traumatized boy still trying to prove he was good enough, a critic ashamed that he smiled at white people when he should've screamed at them; he was a survivor who'd performed for the white gaze for so long that he'd lost track of what was performance and what was him.

In the Western world, that's the unspoken cost of education for people of color. That's how a white supremacist society can appear to offer dreamlike upward mobility when it's actually caulking the seams of its glass ceiling. Through Western education, people of color become professionals with greater economic power, but the trade-off is internalizing a culture that teaches them that they are impostors, that they don't belong, that they must prove their worthiness to white society, and in the most damaging cases, that they are better than the uneducated members of their community. The tradeoff keeps people of color's political power in check. Graduates of this educational system, not unlike the graduates of rehabilitation, pass on their conditioning to the people they love.

"I had to do three times better than the smartest white boy just to get a C in class," my dad used to tell me. My dad taught me what he knew about racism, but he didn't acknowledge that it was something that could hold me back. I just had to develop the right qualities to overcome it. It wasn't just that he thought I could challenge white supremacy through personal excellence; it was that he had no better plan. He didn't have the tools to defeat the imagination problem—that is, he'd lived too long in a country that controlled what solutions he could imagine.

My dad's imagination problem stemmed in part from respectability politics. That term became popular in 1993, the year Professor Evelyn Brooks Higginbotham published her book *Righteous Discontent: The Women's Movement in the Black Baptist Church, 1880–1920*, but long before that, Stokely Carmichael and Charles V. Hamilton called it the "politics of deference." They used it to critique the philosophy of race relations championed by Booker T. Washington in the late nineteenth century in Tuskegee, Alabama. Washington's theory of change deemphasized political activity and taught Black people to believe that if they excelled in education and Black capitalism, they could prove their worthiness. Only then would white people accept Black people as full humans and share political power.[10]

An examination of Washington's theory of change reveals that it didn't bring about equality; it brought an improved living standard for some in exchange for managing the discontent of the many. Washington founded the Tuskegee Institute in 1881, and John D. Rockefeller, J.P. Morgan, and Andrew Carnegie provided generous funding. These men were the richest industrialists in the world; they had become rich and were vested in a system that could not exist without the oppression and death of Black people. Anyone who knows anything about funding knows that these funders were the gatekeepers of the Tuskegee Institute's policies, philosophies, and social objectives. Washington's theory of change wasn't his: in the worst case, his philosophy came from his white supremacist funders; in the best case, his philosophy was what he thought his funders needed to hear to support him. In either case, Washington's theory failed Black people.

Even though my father graduated from medical school, which required working three times as hard as his white peers, he was stopped by the police in 1985 at least once a week driving us to school in the San Francisco Bay Area. He drove a new car. He wore twenty different suits and watches in any given month. He was driving his three sons to the Christian private school whose tuition he could afford. What else could he have done to prove his worth? In American culture, he couldn't *be* worthy, and the police pulled him over every week to show him that a Black doctor was still Black.

They stopped him on the same highway stretch outside the same tunnel each time. Sometimes the police would direct him to get out of the car and put his hands on the hood while they patted him down for weapons they knew he didn't have. They carried out this humiliation without ever acknowledging that my brothers and I were in the car. We would watch through the windshield or crane our necks to look out the back window. My dad resented cops. He, however, always smiled during these encounters, always used the honorific "Officer," and this respectability strategy was part of what it took for a Black person in 1980s America to work hard and play by the rules.

I don't judge my father for perpetuating white supremacy with respectability politics; I understand it in the context of intergenerational trauma responses. Carmichael and Hamilton criticized Tuskegee's respectability politics because they believed the worthiness strategy put too much good faith in white racists. I would argue the opposite: Tuskegee's Black middle class knew all too well who they were dealing with, and their insistence on the politics of respectability was less an outcome of their naivete and more so the rationalization people make to preserve dignity and hope in the face of humiliation. They persisted in the politics of deference because they feared genocide.

They had good reason. In 1866, white people in Louisiana responded to Black freedmen peacefully demonstrating against the Black Codes' disenfranchisement of Black voters with the New Orleans Massacre.[11] Nine years later in the same state, when elections delivered control of a parish government to Black representatives, white people responded with the Colfax Massacre.[12] In 1898, white supremacists in Wilmington,

North Carolina, answered the election of a biracial government with the Wilmington Coup D'état, killing scores of Black citizens and forcing the Black elected officials to flee the city.[13] These kinds of massacres run throughout U.S. history all the way to the Rosewood Massacre in 1923.[14] I don't judge Tuskegee residents any more than I blame my father. This is not a conversation about blame. It's a conversation about what makes a white supremacist, and about the reality that a white supremacist can be as Black as me, yearn for justice for our people like me, and yet behave in ways that undermine our liberation.

My father dedicated his life to the uplift of the Black community. He provided medical treatment to the poor. He employed Black homeless people, going so far as inviting them to live in our home with us. He lost our home and two medical practices because he assumed heavy debt to start a nonprofit that would've provided free education, medical care, and social interventions for Black people in Oakland had it gotten off the ground. And I recognize that he did think less of loud, angry, uneducated Black people, and he did blame them for Black struggle more than he blamed white supremacist institutions like law enforcement. So yes, he smiled in the face of police because he understood who the police were, just as the people of Tuskegee understood the lengths white people would take to compel their deference.

In this way, respectability politics is both a performance for the individual person of color desperate to feel dignity despite feeling powerlessness, and a performance for a white society that demands people of color's self-abnegation in order to assure itself that white dominance is unchallenged.

My older brothers—Eddie and Timi—and I rejected respectability politics, refusing to perform. I can't say why my brothers rebelled. I rejected respectability politics because it was nonsensical, dehumanizing, and enraging. I wasn't afraid enough for it to make sense because my father had protected me from the terror he'd grown up with. In the 1960s, the Black Panther Party had also rejected respectability politics. Instead of petitioning white America for humane treatment, the Black Panthers demanded it. They provided free education, food, medical care, and voter registration services and protected Black communities from police violence. My father witnessed the U.S. government's response. FBI director J. Edgar Hoover circulated a memo that declared the Black Panthers the greatest threat to America and directed his agents to neutralize them and other Black civil rights groups.

According to the FBI's own documentation, the purpose of the agency's unconstitutional activity was clear: "neutralize" included infiltrating groups, sowing misinformation, arresting group members, and assassinating leaders.[15] In one case, the FBI forged documents to create conflicts between the Black

Panthers and another California civil rights group, US Organization, or US. US rejected the cultural definitions of Blackness handed down by white America and sought to create an alternative Black culture by and for Black people. Tension between US and the Black Panthers escalated into a shooting war that opened both groups to deeper criminalization by law enforcement.[16]

Growing up, I'd never heard of US despite knowing about the holiday it had created, Kwanzaa.[17] I grew up in Oakland, the Black Panthers' home base, and the only thing I knew about them were a few black-and-white photos and the words but not the meaning of "Black Power." Adults in my life never talked about it. They thought they were protecting me, that if I knew what the Black Panthers stood for, I might follow in their footsteps and die. Although white kids who rejected their parents' values had punk and other alternative cultures to live out their revolutions, I didn't have a group to turn to like the Black Panthers. I had gangster rap and gang culture.

In 1993, I dropped out of junior high school and joined my brothers in the street-level drug trade, where we made less than $8,000 a year. In a typical week on a street corner, I made $300. I spent half of that to resupply my drug stock. That's $14,400 a year, but factor in the six or more months I spent every year either in jail or quitting the business to avoid jail, and I actually made $7,200 a year. If you also factor in the times I've been pistol-whipped and robbed, the times I destroyed my drugs to avoid arrest, I made less. In 1996, California's minimum wage was $4.75 an hour, or $9,120 annually.[18] I would've made more money working at McDonald's than I did selling drugs. It wasn't a calculated act driven by greed. In the words of Black political philosopher Frantz Fanon, I revolted "simply because I could no longer breathe."[19] Fanon spoke of revolution rather than crime; for Black children like me who were upper-middle class and protected from radical politics, crime was our revolt of choice because armed revolution was a non-option.

When I examine my earliest decisions to break the law, they always came after I experienced an injustice I felt powerless to address. At home, my oldest brother regularly extorted me. My father refused to intervene—he wanted me to stand up for myself. I stood up for myself by stealing money from my brother's bank account. My father found out about it and beat me. I stood up for myself by stealing from him. At an all-white private school I briefly attended in Southern California, a teacher screamed at me and sent me to the principal's office for refusing to take off a Malcolm X T-shirt. I was suspended. I came back and stole the cash box from the school lunchroom. My grandma-ma reported me to the school, and I stole from her.

"They've got *something* for *that*," elders in my community used to say. The "that" was my rage. The "something" was prison or a cop's gun. I didn't listen. To the leaders of my community, my delinquence transformed me from the son of Dr. DeWeaver, the future pride of our respectable race, into one of the loud, angry, more disposable Black people. My elders distanced themselves from me in all the small and big ways that my father distanced himself from undesirable Black stereotypes on the highway. They are the same tactics that Black and Brown leaders practice when assuaging white anxiety. The source of my most traumatic lived experience of my disposable Black body wasn't a cop or a judge or a prosecutor; it was my family, my church, and my community.

Rehabilitation is an iteration of respectability politics. The individual must perform narratives of personal responsibility that deny the known realities of a racist criminal legal system, and rejecting this performance risks having to face all the ways white society employs to destroy dehumanized people. The people I've watched emerge from this performance fall into three categories: those who with varying degrees of success cognitively hold the distinction between their performance and reality; those for whom the distinction collapses and so they become the performance; and those who sense they cannot hold the cognitive dissonance, so they choose to spend the rest of their lives in prison rather than commit spiritual suicide through rehabilitation. People who emerge from performing the politics of respectability fall into similar categories. I've met people who've balanced the cognitive dissonance of respectability with the knowledge that they've sacrificed themselves so that my generation can lay white supremacy bare on the table without being lynched. I've met people who've completely rejected the performance and were denied any chance of social mobility.

We learn about the relationship between rehabilitation and abolition by examining the relationship between respectability politics and white supremacy. Rehabilitation undermines abolition by perpetuating both correctional and white power. Most abolitionists I've worked with know this, but many still use rehabilitation programs in order to have access to incarcerated people. There are merits to rehabilitation, after all, and the public's imagination has been conditioned to assume that something is better than nothing. In reality, this assumption falls apart: gaining no ground is better than losing ground, and rehabilitation perpetuates a cycle of two steps forward, four steps back.

Some abolitionists reject this trade-off by refusing to work within rehabilitation programs or engage in prison reform projects to help incarcerated people, but that can also spell doom for abolition. To see why, imagine a civil rights movement where

Black people stayed home while the rest of America marched across the bridge in Selma, Alabama. Could that work? No. For abolition to work, it must be led not by incarcerated people's families, not by formerly incarcerated people, but by incarcerated people. And incarcerated people can't lead the movement if abolitionists don't rescue them from rehabilitation.

How can abolitionists change the balance of the trade-off? Rather than four steps back, how can they reduce the number of steps back to three, then two, then one? Prison rehabilitation programs aren't necessary to have access to incarcerated people—I talk more in another chapter about the organization I co-founded to prove that fact—but one way that abolitionists using these programs can build more power is to expand the focus, from one solely about access to one that also includes political reeducation, training, and mental support.

What I mean by "mental support" relates to the three groups of people I saw emerge from the rehabilitation process: those who could hold the cognitive dissonance, those who become their performance, and those who rejected the process. I held the dissonance; I have several friends who held the dissonance. And what I noticed about us is that we all had people in our lives who weren't incarcerated to ground us in the reality of who we were rather than who we had to be to get out of prison. These people named that our performances were bullshit, that it was unjust that our lives depended on them. They provided a sacred space for us to speak our full truth if we chose to, and they held that truth for us, skillfully calling us out when we started to forget the truths that we entrusted them with.

By "political reeducation," I mean explicitly teaching incarcerated people the truth about rehabilitation, the strategies and principles white supremacy uses to compel their complicity, and the counter-strategies and principles abolitionists have developed for incarcerated people's liberation. During my time in prison, I watched abolitionists tiptoe around political reeducation, unwilling to recognize an incarcerated person's political views as white supremacist. The abolitionists were justifiably hesitant to tell people who own very little beyond their own beliefs that their beliefs were wrong. Abolitionists working through rehabilitation programs need to find a skillful way to change the balance of the trade-off. If they accept this political reeducation mandate, prison administrators will inevitably root out and expel them, which is why abolitionists must also prioritize training incarcerated people not just to organize themselves but also how to re-educate other incarcerated people and hold their truths. My dream for abolitionists who work inside prisons is that their strategies serve the primary goal of building a collective of abolitionists to fight for themselves while they're in prison.

My dream for abolitionists who will not engage reforms is that they soften the hard lines of this stance. A reform that diminishes parole boards' power to deny parole because the incarcerated person hasn't joined rehabilitation's cult of self-abnegation creates more space for incarcerated leadership. A reform that abolishes prison slave labor specifically by giving incarcerated people the right to own their own labor supports incarcerated people's power to tear down prisons from within. Prisons are small cities, and like cities, they need infrastructure.[20] Millions of people need to be fed three times a day; they need laundry service, electricity, and working toilets. Prisons rely on incarcerated slave laborers; giving incarcerated people labor rights would give them direct power to demand more humane prison conditions.

The Department of Justice reported a total of almost 800,000 working incarcerated people in 2005.[21] That's more than twice the total number of prison guards recorded at that time.[22] Imagine a world where incarcerated people have the political skill of and support from abolitionists, have legislative protection from racist parole boards, and own their own labor. That's a world in which we've shifted the balance of the trade-offs abolitionists often make, and it's a world prisons wouldn't long outlive.

2

Imagination Solutions

In 1998, I was eighteen years old when I shot and killed a man. A year before my trial, I met my newborn child, who now uses they/them pronouns, through a bulletproof glass pane. Their mother sat on a stainless-steel stool, holding them in one of the jail's visiting booths. To their mother, I projected all the hope that I could muster that I'd win my trial—not because I was innocent but because I was a nineteen-year-old whose choices were to either win at trial or die in prison. As I spoke, I watched my sleeping child. Their mom laughed at me and gently shook them awake. Sleepy eyes opened.

"They're so bright!" I said, meaning the whites of their eyes. Those eyes followed me all the way back to my cell. I began to think about what those eyes would see in me as they grew older—what they would be taught to see by their school, the media, and our community. A homeless, junior high school dropout. An absent father. A murderer. One day my child would go to school, and someone would ask them what their dad did for a living. My child would either lie and feel ashamed or tell the truth and feel ashamed. I'd had a love-hate relationship with my own father, so I knew my child couldn't be ashamed of me without also being ashamed of themself. They couldn't grow to hate me without also growing to hate themself.

My kid hadn't been alive one month, and I felt like I'd already killed them. My heart breaking, I curled up on my bunk. I had to get out of prison.

A year later, an Alameda County judge sentenced me to sixty-seven years to life. Mine was one of many lives the state had condemned to end slowly. Elsewhere, as a deputy sheriff hauled me, hobbled and shackled, from the courtroom, a man named Hugo Pinell was serving his twenty-eighth year in a California state prison. He'd been sentenced to seven years to life in 1971. Sandra Davis-Lawrence was serving her twenty-first year in prison. She'd been sentenced to seven years to life in 1982. Marvin Mutch had been sentenced to seven years to life in 1975 for a crime he hadn't committed. An author researching a series of murders discovered evidence of Mutch's innocence and, seven years after my conviction, Mutch presented it to the parole board. That year, 93 percent of people who went before the board to seek parole from life sentences were denied.[1] Mutch received a parole grant, but of the 7 percent of people granted parole, then governor Arnold Schwarzenegger revoked 85 percent of these grants, including Mutch's. This is what "tough on crime" meant in California when I was sentenced to sixty-seven years to life. If you'd asked someone at the time whether I, a junior high school dropout with no social net worth, would walk out of prison twenty-one years later, they would've said, "Impossible." They would have been conflating what we can imagine with what is possible. This is one of the many forms the imagination problem takes.

I ran a workshop in 2019 called The Imagination Challenge for educators, activists, and social scientists who wanted to understand the racialized process of mass incarceration. I talked about how the project of colonialism was partly about the systematic elimination of any ideas in conflict with the perpetuation of Western supremacy, historically expressed as Christian supremacy during the Crusades, European supremacy during the colonialization of Asia and Africa, and finally, during the development of American power through plantation slavery, white supremacy. These iterations of socially engineered ideological norms, which collectively constitute white cultural hegemony, reproduced white supremacist structures that form the bedrock of our contemporary world. Our institutions, from public transit to education to everything else we rely on in childhood to provide our ideological norms, are white supremacist. To put it another way, whether you identify as white or Black or Asian or Latinx, you, your parents, and their grandparents have been taught (with varying degrees of success) to perpetuate white supremacy. And then the people you trust most in this world taught you.

A neuroscientist at my workshop identified the crux of the imagination challenge. When we imagine the future, we rely on the centers in the brain related to memory. This suggests that we can't imagine a world for which we don't have an experiential basis. Our brains store characteristics like the hue of a black olive, the ridged skin of a pineapple, and the smooth texture of a brown leather belt. Because we've experienced these characteristics, we can imagine a ridged black belt even if we've never actually seen one. Without that experience, we can't.

Given the neuroscience, what can we do if all the characteristics we've experienced in contemporary society are white supremist characteristics? Can we imagine the unimaginable? In a word, yes.

Standard procedure in my county jail was that when a person received a life sentence, the administration removed that person from their shared cell and isolated them in solitary confinement, known as "the hole." A sheriff instructed my cellmate to pack my property in a trash bag. He and I were from rival neighborhoods, but the naked oppression of jail had clarified who our allies and enemies were. My cellmate scribbled a note to me that read, "Stay up"—which in our respective neighborhoods meant, *You are strong enough to survive*—and hid the note, along with three books of stamps he gave me (currency in prison), between pictures of my child's birth. While he was writing his goodbyes to me, I leaned my head against my cell door in solitary confinement.

The hole was constructed as a panopticon—concrete, steel, and plexiglass arranged in two tiers around a central well. A guard tower with tinted windows dominated the inner well. A plexiglass partition separated the inner and outer wells, and the latter was further divided by walls into sections called "pods." Each pod had eight or so cells per tier along one wall, two octagonal tables in a recreational dayroom, and a central staircase to the catwalk on the second tier. Beside my head against the door, a rectangle window with wire mesh faced the dayroom. I looked out of my only window to the world at a bank of pay phones. Thinking about calling home, I filled my face with stone to block my tears. Only 20 percent of criminal appeals were successful.[2] My case would not be among them. I had promised my family I would come home, but I didn't know how anymore.

I closed my eyes to escape the seeming truth that I would never get out of prison. But something glimmered in the darkness.

Writing has been my superpower since the fourth grade. For a creative writing assignment, I wrote a story in which what seemed to be a serial killer crept up the stairs while a woman showered (*Halloween* had recently aired on TV). The big reveal: the "killer" was the woman's cat. I had expected to provoke trouble with what I thought was inappropriate material; instead, the teacher kept me after class to say, "Emile, this is amazing." I was a Black boy in an all-white class, and it was the first time someone had ever acknowledged my power.

The second acknowledgment of my power came from my father, and it was the only time I remember him saying, "I'm sorry, son." Putting it kindly, my dad was an unorthodox parent. He was a doctor with three offices in Oakland, so he had the resources to eliminate hardships from our lives. His values and success in life were forged in hardship, however, and he didn't have the imagination to see how we could be successful, ethical people without hardship. So, he manufactured it.

We shopped at bargain centers for five sets of clothes once a year and wore generic shoes to school, because when my father was a kid, he'd had to make do with three sets of clothes. He made us earn money to cover our summer vacation activities (camp, travel, etc.) by hauling bricks from demolition sites in the Bay Area, and he rarely intervened to resolve conflicts in our lives believing we had to learn to be men. The first time I complained of bullying at school, my father strapped oversized boxing gloves onto my hands and made me fight my brother, who outclassed me by forty pounds.

When he fell in love with a woman who moved into our home, his parenting style softened—though only for the woman's son, not for us. The newcomer—I'll call him James— had it easy; my brothers and I hated him because we felt like our dad treated him better than us. My dad seemed to spend more money on James, who was essentially our stepbrother. But James never had to haul bricks with us, and my father constantly intervened to resolve our stepbrother's conflicts with us. We resented James and his mother; we constantly complained to each other about them, but we never complained to our father, because his answer to dissent was a bullwhip he'd bought in Texas. Months later, our resentment hit a boiling point on allowance day.

Every Sunday, after we'd completed chores and homework, we would eagerly line up in my dad's room for allowance. My dad ran a patriarchal household, so he paid us in order of seniority. My oldest brother Eddie received $20; Timi received $10; I received $5. This, of course, didn't feel great for Timi and me, but we bore it as the divine order handed down from the biblical God to Abraham—until the Sunday when our stepbrother joined us in line. My brothers and I shared confused looks because James didn't do chores.

My dad handed out the usual $20, $10, and $5. James's turn came up in line. My father handed him $20. My heart imploded. Timi thinned his lips. Eddie tucked his chin toward his chest, holding his breath. Later, we convened. Someone had to stand up to Dad, and my brothers nominated me, on pain of them kicking my ass if I refused. I wanted to vomit. I couldn't confront my dad in person.

I wrote a letter. I told him that he hurt us. That he always bragged that he'd face Mike Tyson for us, but he was a liar because he treated his girlfriend's son better than us. I left the letter on my dad's nightstand and ran back to my room, where I hid in my closet. Later, when he found me, he was crying. The next day his girlfriend moved back into her own apartment.

Up until that letter, bending my father's will was impossible for me and my brothers because we'd never seen it. A decade later, as I leaned against the window of my cell in solitary confinement, writing was the only thing I'd seen that could achieve the impossible.

I opened my eyes. *I'm going to write my way out of prison.*

On its face, the statement sounds ridiculous, but committing to this possibility taught me the imagination solution. Twenty-one years later, I literally wrote my way out of prison.

The first part of the solution is "radical orientation." Radical orientation is a commitment to a North Star, combined with the emotional discipline to travel only in that direction. When I committed to my North Star, I quit selling and doing drugs, because that lifestyle decision had led me in and out of prison all through my childhood. I stopped gambling because a dice game argument triggered the murder I'd committed. I refused to carry a knife in prison because I practiced quiet pacifism. I took a vow of truth-telling, and I meditated like a Zen monk. I didn't necessarily need all these practices to get out of prison. I ran them like experiments, measuring outcomes by whether they brought me closer to my North Star, and ultimately, this twenty-one-year journey reframed my understanding of possibility.

When someone says something is impossible, they're referring to restrictive conditions at a static point in time—resources, beliefs, or technology—but life isn't static. It exists on a timeline, and time changes all conditions. Take, for example, traveling to the moon. Ancient people couldn't imagine traveling to the moon because, as the neurologist in my workshop observed, experience constrains what's imaginable. Ancient people stared into the sky and saw a mythological object rather than an astrological location. Then someone invented a telescope in 1608, and the moon's identification as a celestial object expanded human vision. People became familiar with the moon as something located in space, to which scientists applied the rules of travel. Over time, the unimaginable evolved into a moon landing, but the moon was *always* a celestial object subject to rules of travel.

Radical orientation is a framework that addresses the limits of our social imagination by focusing on the condition that constrains vision: experience. We travel toward a North Star, as author and community organizer adrienne maree brown writes, one elegant step at a time. We veer off course, learn in community, correct course; and through these processes, we create new experiences that transform our imaginations.

My first elegant step was to learn grammar and craft. I knew the man living next to me in a cell owned the book *The Elements of Style*. I convinced him to let me borrow his book for one day, and in those twenty-four hours, I copied the book by hand onto the blank sides of my court transcripts. I spent the next year hand-copying every kind of book for my writer's library, from Browne and King's *Self-Editing for Fiction Writers* to Budge's translation of *The Egyptian Book of the Dead*.

I became a proficient writer. I followed the advice I'd read: write every day, learn the publishing industry, study the authors you admire, read popular authors to understand your audience, study philosophy, read the classics, study history, study life. I wrote fantasy fiction, a genre I'd loved since childhood, and sent stories to a dozen publishers. The replies rolled in. Most were form rejection letters that read, *Hi, no,* but *come again.* But occasionally, an editor would scribble a note on the form letter offering a word of encouragement or constructive feedback. In publishing, an editor's personal note signals that they see potential in the writer, so I focused on the promise those editors saw, studied their feedback, and rewrote my stories. The rejection letters continued, but with fewer personal notes. I reached my capacity for failure and rejection. Depression halted my writing for a year.

Writing can be a solitary practice, but it still requires a community: people to read your work and help uncover blind spots, moral support from writing groups, mentors to share the lessons they learned over coffee, conventions at which to network. I'd been on a single-minded journey toward my North Star for five years, and my imagination had grown enough for me to see that radical orientation alone would not get me there. I needed community.

I wrote another letter.

I'd been submitting to the L. Ron Hubbard's Writers of the Future Contest every quarter for two years. The back-and-forth of submission, kind rejection, and invitation to try again was the most consistent relationship I had with someone in the free world. I wrote a letter to the contest director, Joni Labaqui, and shared my struggle. *I'm a writer with no community. I can't identify what's missing from my craft alone. Help me.*

Joni returned the kindest (and longest) letter I've received from an editor. *You are not alone. You're miraculous. I've sent you something to read.* Because prison regulations didn't permit her to send me books directly, she tore pages out of a collection on writing essays and mailed them to me. And she continued to remember me, occasionally sending small notes of encouragement. She became the first member of a community invested in my improbable dream. I could tell a dozen versions of a story where a stranger read my words, and that introduction moved them to invest in my dream. Instead of a contest administrator like Joni, I'd tell you about university professors, podcast producers, or philanthropists or advocates or correctional officers.

From these stories, I learned the second part of the imagination solution: collectivity. People often ask me, "How would prison abolition work?" It's a worthwhile question about an ambition that's bigger than my imagination. Some of the brightest minds white supremacy has had to offer developed mass incarceration over decades. Of course, my individual intellect can't offer a comprehensive remedy, but large, complex questions aren't for individuals to answer. They're for collectives with the will and desire to pursue a North Star.

When I published my first story with *The Lascaux Review*, the editors took a special interest in me. Initially, the general sentiment was, *This kid is a beautiful writer and we have to help him succeed*, but our relationships became more than professional. The editors became my family. When I envisioned starting and running a nonprofit from prison, I came to them. They bought the domain name for me and designed the website. My best friend among them, for whom no other title but "sister" feels appropriate, would eventually hire a private attorney for my parole board hearing. There came a point during my time in prison when I gave up contraband cell phones to maximize my chances of going home. That meant having to give up internet access, which meant losing most of my contacts and access to the publishing world. To maintain contact with me, my sister got a prison calling account for collect calls and she, along with a former volunteer at my prison, became my connection to the world. Together, they submitted my stories for me and managed my email accounts. Apart from my sister's support, the owner of *The Lascaux Review* would eventually write my governor a letter of support for my clemency application that stated, "Before I met Emile, I didn't believe in parole. I thought that if you did the crime, you should serve all the time. But if there are other people like Emile in prison, we need to be doing something other than locking them up."

Not everybody knew I was writing my way out of prison, but everybody could see that I fought for radical change in my life. Whatever they saw, they decided mine wasn't a task for one person, so they chose to get involved. Collectivity didn't stop there. The people who stepped up had their own communities. Their friends and family would ask them, "Why are you involved?" The people supporting me would give their answer; their friends and family members would nod, roll up their proverbial sleeves, and join us.

Curtis "Wallstreet" Carroll once rescued me from a bout of self-doubt, saying, "You know you're on the right path when you don't even know the people going to bat for you." Carroll learned to read by studying the *Wall Street Journal* and became a financial wizard who made a lot of money on stock exchanges for prison guards. The relationships his usefulness afforded him gave him access to prison administrators' private conversations. Carroll shared inside information about why I wasn't in the hole after starting a nonprofit organization in prison (an activity that, like organizing, is criminalized in California prisons). He'd been a fly on the wall several times when correctional officers had fought to keep me safe.

Curtis's words shed a new light on several extraordinary moments in my life in prison. In Solano State Prison, I played Dungeons & Dragons with friends. It was more than a game to us; it was how we connected in a place that demanded we perpetually disconnect. I did risky things in order to play that game: I violated racial politics, and I hid in the cells of friends during lock-ups.[3] On one occasion, a notoriously hard-ass correctional officer (complete with buzz cut) caught us. He could have written me up for attempted escape. Instead, he made us agree that we would only gather in a cell on his shift, and that we would tell him ahead of time so he could make sure the officer in the control tower opened the door for us, thus enabling us to return to our cells before headcount time. That typically doesn't happen in prison.

Before Solano, I spent eight years in High Desert State Prison, one of the most violent and racialized prisons at the time in California. I'd come to a point in my life where I was living a vow to do no harm. On the eve of a racial riot between African Americans and Asians, I was standing on one end of the yard with two of my friends, a former cage fighter and a former Crip shot caller who'd made the same vow. The politics of California's maximum-security prisons made participation in a racial riot mandatory: if your race is involved, so are you; you abstain on pain of later being stabbed to death for cowardice. For six years, I'd always managed to be locked in my cell when a racial riot happened, saving me from this decision. My luck had run out. The tear gas began flying.

The former Crip sat down. The former cage fighter—I'll call him Dave—and I looked at each other. First, we pretended confusion, pantomiming like stage actors broadcasting our intentions to the back rows in an effort to buy time. We had intentionally placed ourselves on the opposite end of the yard from the riot, wishfully hoping it would end before we could traverse the divide. I felt my feet moving beneath me. I wanted to hold to my vow. I wanted to go home. More than anything, I wanted to live, so I loped toward the riot as slowly as I could. Dave jogged beside me, we pushed through a corridor of incarcerated people prone on the ground to signal that they were non-participants in the riot. On our right, a riot raged. To our left, a green wall of correctional officers closed in with riot shields and batons. I heard gunshots from an AR-15 assault rifle and dissociated. My only link to my body was the command I gave my legs: don't run faster.

I couldn't run any slower, I couldn't think any quicker. Collectivity saved me. A correctional officer called my name—not my last name, which is the only thing a correctional officer had ever called me at that point. "Emile don't!" he said. I was three-quarters of the way to the riot. I sat down, my ass hitting the ground like a piston. Dave dropped beside me. The wall of green washed over us toward the riot. I was in two kinds of shock, the shock from hearing gunfire and the shock of an officer knowing my first name. People have been booked for riot participation just for standing long enough to survey what's going on before they sit down. Even though officers saw us running toward a riot, Dave and I didn't receive rules violation reports for participation. The bigger problem was that an entire yard had seen us sit down.

After the riot, the correctional officers divided us into bullpens for "skin checks." Skin checks are when guards strip you to examine your skin and knuckles for signs of combat. When someone points a gun at me, it feels like there are pond ripples in my muscles; that's how I felt when I stepped into the bullpen. Dave and I stayed close to each other. We might have just traded violence against Asians in the yard for a fight for our lives with our own people in a cage.

People were sharing stories about the riot—a way of affirming that they'd been involved. Dave was five feet three and known for a peculiar kind of vibe: cheerful with a wolverine's energy lurking beneath his loose, swinging limbs. He turned that energy up full blast and spun a comedic tale about how he and I had lost too much time in our confusion, telling our incarcerated peers that the green wall caught up to us just before we made it to the riot. He told the story as though we'd missed out rather than skipped out, as though we were embarrassed about being idiots rather than deserters. I co-signed with a "Man, that shit was crazy," my voice steady, my heart banging. Our story was ludicrous. And after that, we never heard a word about sitting down during a racial riot.

Collectivity. Just like the editors, advocates, philanthropists, and their communities, countless incarcerated people saw in my task something that inspired them to join my journey. For some, it was through direct support; for others, it was through indirect support, such as turning a blind eye to me sitting down during a racial riot. Another decade would pass before I realized the full extent of collective power working in my life—not until Governor Brown announced he'd forgiven my sentence on the nightly news.

The night of my sentence commutation, men cheered in their cells as though the 49ers had just won the Super Bowl.

It felt fantastic to hear men call out to me with joy in their voices, but I also recognized that they weren't just cheering for me. They were applauding something much more important than me; they celebrated a new experience that had transformed their imaginations.

An incarcerated father spoke to a room of journalists about the effects of my commutation on him. "Before Emile, I wasn't doing anything," he said. "I didn't care . . . I was never going home. Now, I'm going to do something." He wasn't alone in that sentiment; I watched it spread from person to person as people became energized to transform their lives. Their transformations changed the lives around them, just as my journey out of prison rippled through the world around me. With each change, our collective imaginary world grows.

I don't like answering the question about what prison abolition looks like. There's a framing issue in asking the question that ultimately feeds into the imagination challenge, undermining the clarity of any answer I provide. It is possible for the person hearing the answer to understand it and even consider it simple and sensible, but for that to happen, they would need a social, cultural, and political reeducation. What I've learned from radical orientation is that asking the question is a misallocation of our mental resources, because it's not actually important for us to imagine a precise path to a world that doesn't need prisons, and today—just today—it may not be possible. It's enough to want it, to know that we can discover the way tomorrow, and that until we commit to that journey, we're unlikely to grow our imaginations to match the scope of the task. Finally, there's a more powerful question, one to which I yearn to focus the collective brilliance of freedom fighters: How do we build a community whose culture and values will end white supremacy? Because that is the kind of community that will inevitably end prisons.

3

The Lie of Personal Accountability

My father believed in personal accountability. He knew that structural white supremacy existed—he lived with that trauma and passed it to me—but I don't think he believed it was possible to change the world's arrangement with white power. He was brilliant and powerful, but he strategized as someone who felt helpless. To understand what I mean by that, it helps to also understand how this helplessness can manifest in the context of large swaths of the Black community.

I once co-facilitated a public safety conversation in the San Francisco neighborhood of Hunters Point during an upsurge in gun violence. Hunters Point is a predominantly Black neighborhood contaminated by toxic waste.[1] At the time, reeling from the chaos caused by the Covid pandemic, Hunters Point also accounted for half the murders in San Francisco.[2] I'd been called in by an assistant district attorney who wanted to build a restorative justice ecosystem in the city. We both feared that law enforcement supporters would stoke moral panic to do what they often do when violent crime spikes: manipulate residents into making a public outcry in order to surrender more money and power to police.[3]

In the meeting, residents talked about resisting calls for more police and demanding that their public officials invest in services and infrastructure for Hunters Point. This conversation inevitably touched on the influence that white supremacy exerted on their city representatives. After the meeting, I walked by a group of young men discussing their thoughts on organizing to convince public officials to reject white supremacy.

"This is the white man's world," one youth said.

I slowed my step to catch more of the conversation.

"You can get with it, or get run over by it."

This second young man's sentiment lies at the heart of the personal accountability strategy. In Black communities, "personal accountability" isn't just taking responsibility for the harm you commit and not blaming a racist society. It's also accepting that you can't change society, so it's on you to change the way you think and operate in order to survive. For example, if you were to refuse the proverbial Karen's demand to turn off your music in a public park, and then that Karen falsely tells the police you threatened her, leading to the police breaking your arm while arresting you, acolytes of personal accountability would ask, "Why didn't you turn off your music?"[4] According to them, that's the control you had in the situation to avoid escalation. Similarly, when police shot twelve-year-old Tamir Rice to death for playing with a toy gun, a friend of mine expressed disgust not for the police but for the Black parents who would let their child play with a toy gun in a country looking for excuses to kill Black boys.

Personal accountability is often framed as a tool of empowerment, but from my father to the young man in Hunters Point to my friend who blamed Rice's parents for the boy's death, I've always seen concerns about personal accountability begin and end at survival. That it ends solely at survival tells me it grows from a sense of powerlessness.

I became an acolyte of personal accountability in the county jail, the most powerless point in my life. It started when I was twenty years old, reading about karma. A perhaps oversimplified understanding of karma describes a cosmology in which the trajectory of a person's life is the result of their good or bad actions despite there being very little in the modern capitalist world validating this theory. Like Christianity, karmic philosophy resolves this dissonance by dislocating outcomes from our lived world and projecting them into the afterlife or cycles of rebirth.

At the moment of this iteration of personal accountability, I wasn't in jail because of the school-to-prison pipeline, or because the FBI and Central Intelligence Agency had been fomenting the conditions in my community that funneled me into a "kill or be killed" relationship with my victim, or because Nixon had fabricated a war on drugs, or because the media had convinced me through sheer force of saturation that my role in society was as an avatar of white hatred weaponized against Black skin (both mine and my victim's).[5]

I wasn't in jail because of an illegal interrogation that stretched for hours; it wasn't the poverty that denied me fair legal representation; it wasn't the racist judge that coerced a hung jury to change their mind nor the appeals court that ruled such a blatant misuse of judicial power constituted a harmless error. No, I was incarcerated primarily because I had made the wrong decisions. And the U.S. government's concerted efforts to create conditions in which Black people only had bad and worse decisions from which to choose—that was my fault too. In past lives, I must have made decisions that caused me to be born at the bottom of America's caste system.

Although the theory of karma said, *Yes, Emile, your trauma, your limited choices in life, your fate in prison—whether because you made the wrong decisions in this life or another, or because you were too stupid to escape white supremacy's traps—that's the life you've earned for yourself,* it also said, *You have complete power to transform the conditions of your life by the things you choose to do now.* Given my history of trauma, that power to control my world and destiny felt irresistible. It was all the more irresistible because I couldn't see a clear path out of prison, and I would have done anything, believed anything, to feel as though there were a way out.

Incentivized by a belief that my own actions could save me, I radically oriented my life toward becoming the person I wanted to be. At the time, that meant being a father my daughter loved with pride, someone who was compassionate, ethical, educated, reliable, and successful. My father had taught me that literacy was at the heart of education and success, so my journey here, just like my journey to get out of prison, began with my writing life—self-educating, self-discipline, and hand-copying books. When I plateaued and reached out to Joni Labaqui, from the L. Ron Hubbard's Writers of the Future Contest, I struggled with a challenge common to writers. I was hypnotized by the rhythm of my own words when I read them back to myself. In this state, I couldn't tell the difference between what I intended to write and what I'd written. I couldn't tell the difference between the fluidity of the thoughts in my head and those written on the page. Joni helped to break through my depression, but the solution grew from my practice of hand-copying books. I lived and breathed the logics of language and structure; in a moment of inspiration, I realized how to abstract it from the rhythm and flow of words on a page.

I grabbed my latest rejected manuscript, laid it down next to a notebook, and, page by page, I coded the language patterns, literary relations, and grammar structures with numerals and codes. I created a stylometric representation of my written work. I then collected all my favorite authors, past to present, from Kahlil Gibran to George R.R. Martin, coded their works, and compared them to mine. From that analysis, the gap between my plateau and the industry standard emerged. I began to grow again. I coded all my work and, moving forward, incorporated that process into my revision process. I continued growing.

The emotional demands of writing fiction unlocked the empathy at the root of the compassion and ethics that I wanted to show my child. What is more, pattern recognition had become a part of my intellectual vision, and the patterns I recognized were pieces of who I was or who I wanted to be, and it showed up in every compelling character I developed, from hero to villain. In that way, writing fiction was a seed that grew in me both deep self-awareness and an awareness of others' needs and dreams. These qualities led me to the restorative modalities I would later intuit to heal myself and others.

I was becoming who I wanted to be, but then, eleven years into my life sentence, a crisis shifted my gaze from literary structures on the page to the supremacy structures creating the conditions for mass incarceration. At the time, I still battled the bouts of depression inherent to incarceration, but through writing and artistic expression, I had done a significant amount of healing. I felt earthshaking remorse for killing a person, but I'd also forgiven myself. I'd found spiritual grounding in meditation and fasting. I practiced compassion for everyone I engaged with daily, including correctional officers. I'd also graduated from a paralegal course and become both a pro bono jailhouse lawyer for people who struggled with legal literacy and an incarcerated activist challenging conditions of confinement. I'd successfully navigated one of the most violent prisons in California as a closeted pacifist, and I attributed my areas of growth to the reason I had a thriving relationship with my child—they seemed proud of me. In short, I felt at peace with myself, the direction I was going, and believed I had moved on from my past.

My past returned with a double knock on my cell door and a short envelope sliding across my floor. Someone in the same prison but on a separate compound (or "yard," as we say inside) had reached out to me. The letter, or "kite," was contraband, because incarcerated people aren't allowed to write letters to each other without state approval. I flipped the mail open feeling a little less lonely and started reading. I stopped breathing. My heart labored to push oxygen to my brain.

The author was a young man from my neighborhood. I'd never met him, so that meant he was probably an eight-year-old when I went to prison. He told me that the neighborhood still celebrated me eleven years later—a neighborhood I had cut out of my life in my mission to move forward into a new life of redemption. I saw myself in this kid's words, in his hunger to make meaning of the life he'd inherited from a racist country, and it felt clear that he was in prison because for some time now he had been trying to be exactly like me. *I'm his father figure.* The thought transported me back to the county jail, curled up on my bed because I'd felt like I'd killed my child in their first month of life.

I had thought that I'd moved on, that I was at peace with my direction in life, but that illusion was cracked. I could see this kid's future: in and out of prison until the state dropped a life sentence on his bones. If he existed, twenty more boys like him existed that I would never meet. They'd emulate me; a hundred more kids would admire them and follow their path. I trembled as I reread the letter. I was not satisfied. I was not at peace. I was in hell, with no rational sense of why I didn't just kill myself to get some actual peace. I wouldn't wish my life on anyone, not the homicide detectives that fractured my mind in the interrogation room, not the many keepers of my solitary confinement cells over the years, not the racist judge that presided over my case. So, please, God, not this kid.

I panicked. I wrote the kid a preachy letter telling him he had to change his life, that my life was miserable, and, beneath my words, white-hot self-hatred burned the page. It burned the kid too, because he was me. I failed to reach him because I wasn't listening. I was trying to apply an interpersonal solution to a structural problem. The conditions weren't in place for me to save this kid with a sermon that didn't acknowledge even one of the realities of his life. I never heard from him again.

My legacy had been contributing to cycles of violence in my community eleven years after I had broken my own cycle. I had planted a poisonous seed; I resolved to plant the seeds that would heal my community. I became involved in advocacy, and the structure-focused vision I'd developed as a writer became a tool for transformative justice. I moved from writing fantasy fiction to writing about social issues. I became a journalist challenging the harmful narratives that cultural hegemony forces people to accept as common sense. I became an advocate devoted to abolition and community healing. I developed a platform for my voice so that I could be a different kind of role model in my community.

This is where my personal accountability narrative can become dangerous. A familiar energy takes over rooms of both liberals and conservatives when they hear my story. Hands go up, and the questions presuppose that there's a formula in my decisions that listeners can mine for their program ideas to solve poverty or mass incarceration or climate change. They clap when I talk about the need for culture change, but their questions often reveal to me that the culture they're thinking about is mine, that when I left street culture (read: Black culture) behind, my life transformed, and that change is the source of my empowerment. They hear proof that personal accountability works, because it is true that accountability fueled many of my actions, and those actions have resulted in key structural changes.[6] It's also true that people should be accountable, but these facts obscure some truths.

We can't use the strategies available in my story to define social justice strategy. I'm proud of the personal victories in my life—they're miracles—but to justify a personal accountability strategy using my story is an attempt to resolve the harms of mass incarceration and white supremacy by requiring the majority of non-white people to become miracle workers. That defies the meaning of *miracle*, which is partly defined by rarity. Committing to such a strategy is also an admission of comfort with the white supremacist arrangement given that we don't put these same superhuman expectations on white people. In short, personal accountability as a strategy for racial or class justice not only fails to acknowledge white supremacy, it strengthens the power structure because it concedes that the structure can't be changed. In the words of the young man from Hunters Point, "get with it, or get run over by it."

My father used to beat me for failing to be excellent. Afterward, he would sit me down and say, "I'm hard on you, son, because you have to be twice as good as any white boy to make it in this world." I remember how humiliated I felt for myself and my father. *Inequity is wrong, but that's just how the world works today*, we tell ourselves in our heads. Our minds know we're just as good, but something else is happening in our body that undermines our spiritual power. I learned this in generative somatic therapy, a branch of healing that holds, in colloquial terms, that the physiological body has its own version of mental health that requires treatment. The body remembers trauma, so people seeking treatment need a more holistic approach than that offered in talk therapy. One piece of wisdom that somatic theory reveals is that the body doesn't know the difference between a lie and the truth. Everything is true to the body. So, there was no way I could strive twice as hard as my white peers and not teach my body that I was worth half as much. What my father asked me to do is what we're asking when we teach people to lift themselves out of a broken system by their bootstraps.

The bootstrap philosophy obscures several more truths. One, "lifting yourself up" is as much about what you're lifting yourself out of as it is about where you land. In my case, the story that is often recoded from my story by white minds is that I had to get out of Black culture. No one would say that, of course. They'd call it "poverty culture," "gang culture," or a "criminal mindset"; but every instance of these dog whistles I've heard refers to Black and Brown cultures. People who've yet to examine how whiteness colors their moral lens often applaud my story more for what I seem to have left behind than for the fact that I've escaped a civil death sentence. For them, a narrative in which I've escaped the influence of my Black culture to speak and write their language better than them, for the edification of their children in elite universities I cannot (and do not want to) attend, legitimates white cultural hegemony, the idea that the white way is the right and natural one. They're living the present-day iteration of the missionary's justification for enslaving, murdering, and brainwashing continents of people: to save savages from their own inferior cultures. This lie gives them a way to cling to an idea of justice that doesn't require them to relinquish their privilege, which lies at the root of injustice. It gives them a free pass to forgo radical action and tell their children that the perpetual suffering of Black and Brown people in this country doesn't come from their children's stolen privilege. It comes instead from non-white culture and the decisions individuals make because of their culture.

They would point to someone like me, like my father, and say, "See, they didn't let their rotten conditions define their choices. They have hardships, they have trauma, but they don't turn to crime. They make the right decisions."

Personal accountability narratives have a penchant for cherry-picking examples of people who are presented with good choices to make. I began to make better choices after my child's birth, but conditions had as much sway over my possibilities as they did for the kid who wrote me a letter in prison and the thousands of young men pouring into prisons on the same day the governor released me.

When I was a kid, my culture was often compared by both white and Black people to crabs in a barrel. According to the analogy, if you put crabs in a barrel, they'll all die because they compete to get out. When one crab reaches the lip of the barrel, other crabs pull it back down. It describes a culture based on the negative reinforcement of success. Popular media often ascribes this process to Black communities with narratives about gangs violently pressuring Black youth to join them. Based on belief in this phenomenon, the state discourages contact between incarcerated people and all their former friends (and sometimes even their mothers and fathers). Based on this belief, people in prison hide their good fortune from others (from a pending visit from a family member to a parole date) for fear of being pulled back into the barrel. I believed this myself. It was one reason I severed my relationships with people from my neighborhood during my first decade in prison. Then, the governor's office announced my commutation on the local news and the cellblock erupted with some of the most joyous celebration I've ever heard. That moment forced me to look back on my life and reassess my gang history.

I'd been selling drugs with a street gang since I was a fourteen-year-old homeless kid, and the longer I did it, of course, the deeper I fell into a life with a different set of rules than that of my father's world. By the time I was arrested for murder four years later, I occupied a leadership position. That might be the story a television show would portray about a promising Black kid lost to the ghetto. What it would be leaving out is the efforts my gang took to keep me off the street.

I slept in their homes; I ate their food. When I started selling crack, they would chase me off the neighborhood block, screaming, "Take your little ass to school" or "Take your little ass home!" When it became clear that I wouldn't be deterred from street life (and perhaps that I wasn't going home and I needed income), the older guys in my neighborhood (twenty-one and twenty-two years old) offered me a deal. I had permission to sell drugs on the block but not during school hours. They acknowledged that they weren't my father and couldn't make me go to school, but selling dope wouldn't be the reason I wasn't at school. In me, they saw a potential that Black people in my community have been validating all my life. They saw the son of a doctor who could go to college and build a stable, happy life. They saw all the things they didn't believe they could have for themselves, and, in their imperfect ways, they were trying to protect my future. This would continue through my entire stay in prison.

In the county jail while I awaited trial, I lived with an active member of the Black Guerrilla Family (BGF), a militant arm of the Black Panthers founded by activist George Jackson. All government documentation of this group portrays its members as demonic cop killers who are such a threat to prison security that during my time in prison, a person could be locked in solitary confinement forever for no other reason than being a member. My cellmate was a skeletal man in his fifties with fingertips that were blunt and burned from hard labor and the hot glass of crack pipes. He'd been a high-ranking BGF member and a prison hit man decades ago, so being recruited by him would have given me instant power and prestige. I was a depressed teenager with father issues facing sixty-seven years to life. My despair and hunger for validation would have made me a perfect soldier for his cause. But instead of recruiting me, he spent nights in our cell teaching me how someone could go to prison and never need to join a gang. He taught me how to build a reputation that would protect me from violence and minimize conflict. He saved my life like the men from my neighborhood tried to save me, like even the acolytes of respectability tried to save me.

In teaching me how to navigate prisons, avoid conflict, and remain safe, he made it possible for me to write myself out of prison.

What other conditions allowed me to pursue my dream?

After prison guards killed George Jackson in 1971, BGF underwent the same process many supranational political bodies that are both hierarchal and violent went through. When Alexander the Great died, his empire and vision fell to chaos; Julius Caesar died, chaos; King Charlemagne, chaos. Many people had joined BGF to protect Black people in prison from the white supremacist guards who were killing them. After Jackson's death, many began to prey on other

Black people, and a new gang arose in response. Men from the Bay Area founded a political body called 415 in the 1980s with a mission to protect incarcerated people from the Bay Area from predation. Despite 415's mandate to protect vulnerable people, state narratives portrayed the group as posing the same threat as BGF, and verification of membership also could mean an indefinite term in solitary confinement.

Twenty years after 415's founding, I arrived in prison a brainy Black kid from Oakland whose rejection of gangs and prison politics meant he didn't present as "tough." If my story were portrayed on television, I would be that stereotypical kid victimized in prison or harassed in school hallways by the crabs in a barrel who can't stand the sight of someone with the promise they believed they lacked themselves. In reality, I served a twenty-one-year prison term without ever having to "prove myself" with an act of physical violence, and did so without ever being assaulted for being soft. This gang protected me. I didn't ask for it. They didn't ask me for anything; we never even had a conversation about it outside of the casual, "You okay, youngster?" "You got food, you need anything, youngster?"

This is not to romanticize underworld political organizations. They are unquestionably violent because they operate in the violent worlds imposed on them by a white supremacist capitalist system. Not even international organizations trying to end world hunger always live up to their founding values. The mission of a political body in prison operated by men drowning in trauma is no different. The group's existence didn't guarantee my safety even from its members, but my co-defendant and I had chosen each other as brothers. He's in prison because he saved me from being shot to death. He's a natural caretaker, so when he came to prison he joined 415, drawn by its mission to protect Black people. He became important in 415, so the fact that I was his little brother was another reason I could be a weird Black kid practicing pacifism in one of the most violent prisons in California. That, combined with the lessons I'd learned from my cellmate in the county jail, gave me a reputational standing in prison that made me unassailable as long as I didn't violate prison decorum.

But then I violated decorum by sitting down, along with Dave, during the racial riot between African Americans and Asians. I violated the mutual defense pact that keeps so many people safer than they'd otherwise be. For this, someone from Oakland should have disciplined me—that is, they should've stabbed me. In virtually any other scenario, no influence from 415 could have prevented this act of discipline. No amount of respect for my brother exempted me from this rule, and no reputation could have survived this perceived cowardice. The entire yard turned a blind eye to my betrayal, betrayed their own vision of justice, because they wanted me to succeed at this thing that I was doing—even though they didn't understand what I was doing.

What other conditions made it possible for me to write my way out of prison?

An infamous jewel thief from San Francisco moved into my cell. He taught me the most important lesson of my life: "Emile, no one should ever meet you and come away worse off. They should break even or be better off." This was the lesson in relationship-building responsible for every success I've had in my professional and political life. Another man, a mentor of mine at the *San Quentin News*, had worked for Pacific Bell for decades before prison. He laid bare the white power structures in the professional world, and from his stories, I learned how to navigate capitalism.

Why did so many men fight for me to live and survive? At least one reason was the selflessness of my father. My dad was both a horrible husband and father, but he gave everything to the Black community he yearned to save. He was a doctor, but he died broke because his patients had little money to pay. I've come home many times to find a homeless man sleeping on our couch. My dad would give these men work around the house, and although I resented my father because he seemed to take better care of strangers than he did his children, I can't count the times I've run into complete strangers who would do anything for me because they love my father. The man in the county jail knew my father. I hadn't realized it at the time, but people in prison knew my father because they came from the communities to which he gave his everything. All my life, the people trapped in the barrel with me haven't been pulling me down. They've been giving me their backs to climb out. That's Black culture.

Ironically, the comparison between Black communities and crabs in a barrel holds, but not in the way we've been taught. Animal researchers found that crabs, in fact, cooperate to escape barrels.[7] In one experiment, after researchers placed a group of crabs in a barrel with a narrow opening, they found that the crabs would help each other climb out. Forming a line, each crab would pull the one behind them up through the opening.

What the facts of my personal transformation often obscure are the people who made my change possible. There were conditions in place that had nothing to do with my personal power but that made it possible for me to manifest my dream. When we miss that part of the story, we fail to grasp that the conditions are what we must work to change, not the people in them. We fail to see that we need collectivity to change those conditions. Everyone wants to do well. I've never met someone in prison who said, "I want to come back to prison." Everyone leaves wanting to succeed, but if the right conditions don't exist, they won't.

4

A Fight to Build Power

I love the stage. In prison, I performed Shakespeare, directed my own original pieces, danced, jammed on guitars. During my first guitar solo in a yard show, an incarcerated person ran figure eights around the stage, arms stretched like an airplane. I watched him, grinning. I'd done that. Euphoric. Most of my life, I've struggled to feel seen, and it left a hole that needed to be filled by other people's love and validation. The nonprofit organizations that run many prison programs exploit this hole. I don't think they do this intentionally; blinded by the imagination problem, they think they're empowering incarcerated people.

I believe Marin Shakespeare is one such organization. It's a theater arts nonprofit organization founded in 1989 by a white woman living in Marin, one of the wealthiest counties in California. In 2003, the organization began running its prison programs, which it describes on its website as programs that fuse drama and therapy by hosting stage productions with the goal of inspiring the public to fix prisons by redressing the racialized mechanisms that feed mass incarceration.[1] I joined its Shakespeare in Prison program, which gave incarcerated people an opportunity to write and perform stage plays in prisons for a public audience. I learned new skills from other incarcerated actors, formed lifelong bonds, and drank in the crowd's applause. The program allowed me to experience the connection I needed, and the impact of my performances and endorsements of Marin Shakespeare helped it generate donations. I happily made this trade-off, enjoying the benefits of feeling seen and celebrated, but that doesn't mean I wasn't exploited.

One incarcerated actor shared a story with me that drove home how exploited I felt. During a Marin Shakespeare performance, this friend of mine, a Black man, brilliantly performed his life story. He left his heart on that stage. The founder of Marin Shakespeare sat in the audience next to a wealthy woman from Marin. Emotion trembled in this donor's voice as she spoke to the founder. She'd never seen anything like this performance before. She had witnessed my friend's struggles as a youth, his triumphs as an adult, glimpsed the hardships ahead that he faced, and her heart broke for him.

She said to the founder, "That was amazing. How can I help you?" This woman had the power to change my friend's life forever, but she responded to his gift to her not by asking how she might support my friend or people like him. Instead, she wanted to know how she could support another white woman's power. Her response suggests to me that this donor can't trust my friend to help himself with her resources, but somehow because of him, she trusts the white-led organization. The founder told the woman how she could help the organization as my friend basked in the adoration of his audience. And that's all he was left with: he'd been reduced to an instrument to expand the resources of a white organization. Instrumentalization of those in a lower hierarchal position to grow the resources of a white institution—that's white supremacy.

Neither the women in the audience discussing fundraising nor my friend likely think about this injustice in terms of instrumentalization or white supremacy—or even as an injustice. I know the founder; she's a good woman who wants a more just world. Both she and my friend are mired in that version of the imagination problem where they believe they're resisting oppression but are actually digging a moat around the oppressor's citadel. In their minds, they're humanizing and empowering incarcerated people, democratizing liberal arts access, lowering recidivism, promoting public safety: they're acting on narratives (and logics) they've inherited from a social justice machine oiled by white hegemony.

Effective narratives can hypnotize us and bypass our critical minds. This presents a challenge for advocates and nonprofits similar to the one I faced as a young writer when I was hypnotized reading my own words. Unable to tell the difference between what I intended to write and what I'd written, I broke the spell by creating a stylometric system to abstract my words from the page. When it comes to social justice strategy, policy design, and nonprofit programs, we need a similar tool to get out of our heads and better communicate with each other about the social interventions we support. I developed such a tool to better understand how programs like Marin Shakespeare perpetuate white supremacy and to discern how I might design alternatives.

The tool is a thought exercise that first imagines a scenario and an intervention. Then it measures the distribution of power among the scenario's stakeholders before the intervention and after it, and then analyzes the outcomes of that power redistribution in terms of the stated aims of the intervention. For example, if the stated aim is to address mass incarceration, but the intervention diverts power from incarcerated people and their families to the prison system, then it is clear that what seemed like a good intervention is a near enemy. This tool relies on the premise that an analysis of white supremacy is an analysis of structural power, and that we can tell whether something is white supremacist by whether it strengthens or weakens the white power structure. To investigate this, I'll create a map of a system that charts how I see power move through it, and then I apply a zero-sum analysis.

Economists and strategists apply a zero-sum analysis to scenarios entailing limited resources, where one party's gain means another party's loss.[2] It's called "zero-sum" because the total gains and losses among participants add up to zero. Every analysis of power needn't be zero-sum, but it suits conversations about social justice because the entities that carry out social justice activities, whether they're nonprofit organizations, media companies, or civil services agencies, operate on service models with limited resources. In my analysis, I measure services by resources provided, and, regardless of whether they're material, emotional, or temporal (such as labor, for example), these resources are always limited.

When I've observed activists and organizations design interventions without a zero-sum lens, they will initially feel positive about the intervention in the short term, but then come to regret the unforeseen long-term outcomes. Take developments in recent years in bail reform, a social justice movement that opposes detaining people in jails because they can't afford to pay thousands of dollars, even though they are presumed innocent. Leaders in this movement have fought against a racist legal system that incarcerated people essentially because they are poor. The eventual intervention resulted in a legal system that relies on racist "flight risk" algorithms that disproportionately incarcerate poor people of color.[3]

Explaining why this happened deserves its own book, but, after having had a front seat from which I watched peers of mine who led bail reform grow more and more alarmed at the direction the reform took, I'd argue that the unintended outcomes arose from at least two factors. Advocates—not all of them, but those with the funding that gave them the loudest voices—focused on the increased freedom they envisioned poor people would get without much thought about what the legal system responsible for the injustice would lose in return. State legislators who listened to these advocates took power from bail bondsmen by abolishing cash bail without hesitating to deliver that power to the racist legal system responsible for the injustice. A zero-sum analysis that follows the distribution of power might have laid this absurdity bare in the development stage, but instead legislators missed the point of bail reform. Although bail bondsmen were parasites in an unjust system, the root injustice wasn't that courts could detain people because they were poor. It was that they could detain people, sometimes for years, even though they were innocent until proven guilty under the law.

Before I trace the distribution of power, I construct a point system. For the sake of simplicity, I use a 10-point system, distributing these points among the stakeholders affected by the intervention and those responsible for it. I assign the greatest number of points to the stakeholder with the most power, and then I assign the rest proportionately, based on how powerful I think a group or organization is in relation to the most powerful stakeholder. People using this tool might assign different numbers than I would. The initial assignments are imprecise, and that's okay for two reasons. One, the points are only a placeholder for the broader idea of "more power or less power," so they need only approximate a reasonable reflection of a person's understanding of stakeholders. Two, the tool's principal purpose is to help measure the dispersal of power—that is, who's losing for someone else to gain.

In the case of my Marin Shakespeare example, the stakeholders are the prison system, the philanthropic community that funds Marin Shakespeare, Marin Shakespeare itself, and incarcerated people. As the legal authority who ultimately decides whether Marin Shakespeare can run its program, the prison has the most structural power. I assign them 4 points. The philanthropic community has no legal power, so it has less power than the prison but more than Marin Shakespeare because the latter relies on philanthropic support. I assign the philanthropic community 3 points. Marin Shakespeare has more power than the incarcerated people who rely on the nonprofit, so I assign Marin Shakespeare 2 points. That leaves 1 point to give incarcerated people. Marin Shakespeare wants change in incarcerated people's lives and change in the prison system, but when I examine how power moves between the stakeholders, I see an organization that takes power from incarcerated people and delivers it to prisons.

When a warden gives Marin Shakespeare access to a prison, it's a point of power delivered to Marin Shakespeare, but it's delivered more like a loan than a gift. When the prison opens its gates for the voting public to come inside and watch a live performance by incarcerated artists, Marin Shakespeare will praise the prison's enlightened approach to incarceration. I've participated in and watched dozens of public events hosted in prisons featuring nonprofit organizations, and the organizations' staff members always thank the warden and publicly extol his progressive values. I've talked to nonprofit staff members about why they do this. Some believe that if they focus on the positive things wardens do, it will encourage them to support more of the organizations' program ideas. Others admit they're playing to a warden's political ambitions: if staff members make the prison look good, the warden, hungry for a promotion, also looks good. This praise increases the prison's social and political capital—and that's why I say Marin Shakespeare gets a point from the prison but gives it right back.

In fact, the organization pays it with interest, because Marin Shakespeare incorporates the lie of rehabilitation into its programming. While I don't know whether it incorporates the lie with malicious intent, its stated aim of personal growth for incarcerated people and fixing the prison system misaligns with the outcomes it creates. It covers its interest payment to the prison system by taking a point from the incarcerated people, who've been indoctrinated by a lie that strengthens the very system that harms them and other incarcerated people.

Taking incarcerated people's power doesn't stop there, because incarcerated people perform in Marin Shakespeare productions for audiences that include big donors. I know they include big donors because I've met them, heard them talk about their support for Marin Shakespeare, and even though it's against prison rules to use these events to raise money, another friend of mine and I thrilled at the prospect of moving through these crowds after the show. I imagine that we weren't the only ones. We praised Marin Shakespeare without ever being asked to, without ever mentioning money, in the belief that the more rich people we won with our personalities, the more they would donate to Marin Shakespeare. That's a point going from the philanthropic community to Marin Shakespeare.

Our promotion of Marin Shakespeare was our way of showing gratitude, of loving the people who were kind to us, but feeling thrilled, grateful, and willing doesn't protect people from exploitation. That's a point transferred from incarcerated people to Marin Shakespeare, because we weren't paid for our performance on stage or our promotion off stage, in accordance with prison policy—a policy that undergirds slave labor in prison. The lie of rehabilitation had taught us that we were contributing back to society for all we had taken with our crimes, following the same logic that justifies why prisons should be able to force incarcerated people to work without pay.

Extracting from incarcerated people wasn't the only thing Marin Shakespeare did. It taught us performing arts. It gave us a craft that inspired pride, joy, and, for some people, personal healing. That's something—a point from Marin Shakespeare to incarcerated people. But these benefits live in the realm of personal, not structural, power. Ask any number of incarcerated people involved in Marin Shakespeare, and many will give a rave review. They've felt their personal power grow, but the benefits that accrued to the prison system are primarily structural power. Two decades as an activist have taught me that when it comes to social change or social stratification, structural power outweighs personal power. When I look at Marin Shakespeare's intervention, I see a scenario in which the prison system begins with the most structural power and ends with even more of it.[4]

This is how I've seen the interventions of most prison programs work, because no matter who runs them, their continued access to prison relies on them adopting the prison's logics. In other words, nonprofits like Marin Shakespeare become extensions of the prison machine. To understand what I see in these nonprofits, consider solitary confinement. It's easy to see what's wrong with solitary confinement, how its isolation and deprivations destroy people's lives, but I see a disconnect in conversations about the practice. I suspect that a significant number of people who protest solitary confinement on humane grounds don't also protest the existence of prison. Yet, prison *is* solitary confinement in the sense that the same inhumanity and harms we attribute to solitary confinement can also be attributed to prison. The first prison in the U.S., Eastern State Penitentiary, was, in fact, opened in 1829 to be a solitary confinement experience.[5] The Quakers, who proposed the penitentiary system, thought that a strategy based on isolation with a Bible would prevent crime. It proved catastrophic, and the penitentiary's strict confinement practices ended around 1871. Deemed a failure, it closed a hundred years later, but the function and architecture of prisons have not significantly changed since then. Through the combination of its original structure and its administrative rules, prisons have, in fact, evolved to be more effective at isolating people. The processes that operate in solitary confinement also operate throughout the rest of the prison. The difference between them is one of scale and intensity, but what we're talking about is like the difference between three cigarettes a day and ten. While we can acknowledge that that's an important difference, we can also unequivocally say the cancer patient's ultimate goal is to stop smoking, not to reduce their daily habit from ten to three cigarettes.

Those same processes operating in prison also operate in the rehabilitation programs that nonprofit organizations and private citizens run in prisons. Marin Shakespeare is but one of many. Alliance for CHANGE provides reentry support while teaching restorative justice principles. Guiding Rage Into

Power teaches mindfulness and emotional intelligence. Insight Prison Project offers its Victim Offender Education Group program, a cognitive behavioral initiative designed to foster empathy, remorse, and personal accountability in incarcerated people. All these programs have merit, but like prisons, they rely on incarcerated people's slave labor. They introduce skilled volunteers (often graduate students working for school credit) to make the initial investment of teaching their skills to a group of incarcerated people, who then carry on the work of designing curricula and facilitating self-help groups, a broad category that encompasses everything from arts programs to rehabilitation programs. Although the volunteers stay on to supervise, the incarcerated people become the leaders and change agents in these scenarios, but the hosting nonprofit organizations reap the benefits—the funding, the accolades—for the incarcerated leaders' work. The organizations' staff and volunteers feel compelled to take the credit to protect their service population because the prison system's rules—written and unwritten—disallow incarcerated leadership. Prisons regularly send incarcerated leaders to solitary confinement. Prisons have the authority to approve fair compensation for incarcerated people's labor; they don't, and would end any nonprofit organization's program that did.

Like prisons, nonprofits that run programs inside of prisons perpetuate a culture of isolation. That acculturation begins immediately with the orientation class provided by the prison that nonprofit staff and volunteers must complete. I've talked to the participants about these orientations, which push propaganda convincing them that, since they don't know which incarcerated person is the "bad apple," they have to be hypervigilant with all of them. Nonprofit staff enter the prison with that first impression, and then must double down on this culture of isolation because they're bound by the same rules that regulate guards' interactions with incarcerated people. Nonprofit staff encourage incarcerated people to be vulnerable, to share about their lives, but they can't reciprocate that vulnerability. If they do reciprocate, they can be expelled from the program, and the incarcerated person can be charged with "overfamiliarity." To be found being overfamiliar in prison is a nebulous charge that can mean whatever a correctional officer wants it to mean, but it essentially establishes that the incarcerated person has fostered a personal relationship with a prison volunteer or staff member—not the other way around, as the regulation frames it.[6] This charge can be proven based on evidence as flimsy as the incarcerated population's perception (i.e., rumor), and it doesn't need to be a romantic or sexual relationship; *any* personal, human relationship is against the rules in prison. So, to safeguard their programs from human relationships, nonprofits teach their volunteers that they can't trust incarcerated people with personal information—where they're from, their hobbies, their dreams, their struggles, what they're watching on TV.

Like prisons, nonprofits that run programs inside of prisons often teach incarcerated people to hate themselves while calling it "healing" or "accountability," because that's how the lie of rehabilitation works. These organizations win access to a prison based on the premise that they're coming in to teach the prison's vision of rehabilitation. Over the course of twenty-one years, only three times did I see organizations ostensibly support the prison's vision of rehabilitation for access while secretly attempting to do radical work. More often, I found myself sitting in rehabilitation classes and observing that although the incarcerated leaders talked about healing, the paths to restoration that they described centered self-hatred, self-negation, and the lie of personal accountability. Another imagination problem.

When I'm trying to solve an imagination problem, I often arrive at the question: How do I create a new experience that presents wider possibilities? People accept how nonprofits operate in prison because they don't see another way. When I speak to nonprofit executives about why they perpetuated a culture of isolation or slave labor or prison administrators' power, invariably the answer is that they had to. They can't center human relationships because it's dangerous—an incarcerated person might manipulate a volunteer into doing something illegal. They can't pay incarcerated people for their labor because that's against prison rules. They have to praise prison administrators because that show of gratitude maintains nonprofits' access to the incarcerated people whom organizations want to help.

One consequence of cultural hegemony is that we're all situated within harmful systems—from the criminal justice system to capitalism, patriarchy, and white supremacy. It's the world we've inherited, and it is the only place from which many can start their work. The question arising from this is: What's the goal of the work you're doing, and how does that goal redistribute power from those who've misused or stolen power to the people you serve? If you could repeat your work over successive iterations, can you see how the outcomes could accumulate in a way that makes the current power structure unsustainable?

How do I redistribute power and how do I create a new experience to resolve an imagination problem? These were the questions I wanted to answer in 2015 when I co-founded Prison Renaissance from my prison cell. Prison Renaissance was ostensibly an arts and education nonprofit for incarcerated creatives who wanted a platform for their work. Beneath this surface-level branding, however, we were also a hub for incarcerated leaders to organize around political issues more safely—since organizing in prison is illegal. The arts gave us

First Amendment protections, which allowed us to operate in prison whether the state approved or not. Independence would allow us to undermine slave labor by paying incarcerated artists, support those incarcerated leaders who wanted to use their art as part of larger political strategies, and challenge the culture of isolation by facilitating lifelong relationships between our incarcerated artists and free volunteers.

This latter goal came from our commitment to use strategies that would eventually make us unnecessary, a vital component of any program seeking to actually redistribute power to the people it serves. For example, our programs centered models in which incarcerated and free people developed and executed a project together. Traditional nonprofits in prison maintain a mediating position, serving as a middleperson between the incarcerated person and the free volunteer. The incarcerated person can't contact or work with free volunteers without the nonprofit's involvement, and vice versa. Prison Renaissance provided guidance but ultimately required participants to communicate and build relationships with each other directly, so that when a project was complete, participants could either continue working with us or take the relationships they'd built through our projects and continue without us.

We began with an online journal publishing incarcerated people's writing and art. We expanded to incorporate incarcerated people's writings into college curricula, and this led to

Prison Renaissance at Stanford, an annual zine project where incarcerated people and undergraduates designed narrative projects about issues important to them. Soon, Prison Renaissance facilitated guest lectures given over the phone by incarcerated people at Stanford, UC Berkeley, and in other universities across the country. In 2018, we hosted the first live arts exhibition in San Francisco curated and run by incarcerated people. We called it Metropolis because at the time the U.S. incarcerated more people than the entire population of Houston. It featured audio installations where audiences listened to incarcerated people's stories and live events where incarcerated people facilitated a workshop, community conversation, and poetry exchange through a phone piped through Bluetooth speakers.

Our interventions created new models for how organizations can serve incarcerated people without exploiting them or consolidating prisons' power over our social imaginations. Seeing this strategy in action, a handful of nonprofit organizations in the San Francisco Bay Area changed the way they did business: the Ella Baker Center for Human Rights, a strategy and action center that organizes to pass legislative policies that decarcerate and support urban communities; UnCommon Law, which supports incarcerated people in navigating parole boards; and the Prison Law Office, which defends the constitutional rights of incarcerated people. They all adopted Prison Renaissance's strategies to incorporate incarcerated people into their organizational activities, and they paid incarcerated people for their labor. Other organizations have adopted Prison Renaissance's language, but I haven't worked with them or studied their program outcomes to know whether they actually adopted our strategies or defaulted to their near enemies. Whatever the case for these organizations, I still consider Prison Renaissance's model a victory over the imagination problem because even if organizations are creating near enemies, that indicates that our model has shifted public consensus on what the ethical ways to serve incarcerated people are.

I also consider it a victory because I can verify it by following the redistribution of power. The stakeholders are the prison system (which initially has 4 points), the philanthropic community (3 points), the general public (1 point), Prison Renaissance (1 point), and incarcerated people (1 point). The money Prison Renaissance raises is a point of power taken from the philanthropic community, because financial resources are power. Our programs disrupt prison slave labor and disrupt the prisons' role as gatekeeper for nonprofits' prison programs, which equates to a point of power taken from the prison system because it reduces its control. Prison Renaissance invests its resources in a platform that pays incarcerated creatives and activists to work toward their goals. The compensation amounts to 1 point moving from Prison Renaissance to incarcerated people, and the platform that supports their professional and personal networks is another.

In turn, incarcerated people invest their resources—time and talent—in both literary and political projects that show the public a clearer picture of incarceration and incarcerated people. A clearer picture fosters an expanded public imagination, which undermines the prison system's ability to perpetuate a false narrative about criminal justice. The power the general public receives, then, amounts to 2 points—one from incarcerated people's efforts and another representing the narrative power that prisons have lost.

At the end of Prison Renaissance's intervention, the prison system has lost 2 points of power; the philanthropic community has lost 1; the general public has gained 2; incarcerated people have gained 1; and Prison Renaissance has netted zero.[7] If Prison Renaissance were to successfully duplicate our work over and over, the outcomes could result in the accumulation of enough power to disrupt mass incarceration while empowering incarcerated people to have control over their lives. This is an example of how to work for incarcerated people without becoming an extension of the very system that oppresses them.

When I co-founded Prison Renaissance, I was in my second year working for the *San Quentin News* (*SQN*), the prison's newspaper and crown jewel of San Quentin's rehabilitation brand. It was run by incarcerated people and supervised by the prison's public information officer and volunteer editors from the journalism world. At the time, *SQN* branded itself as "the voice of the voiceless," with the intention of representing incarcerated people who are traditionally silenced by state structures. Initially, the mission inspired me, but the more I grew politically, the more I saw that *SQN*, like other prison programs, was an extension of the state. I came to understand that it did not represent the voice of incarcerated people but instead represented the voice of the state. I saw this reality play out countless times, as we supposedly had the power to "print anything we wanted," yet I also sat in the meetings where we censored ourselves, staying away from reporting on subjects that would upset our administrative benefactors. We were in the same position as nonprofit organizations who have to remain in prison administrators' good graces to preserve the privilege of running their program.

It might seem counterintuitive for me to say that *SQN* was the voice of the state if you're familiar with California's tough-on-crime narratives because *SQN* unequivocally rejected that approach in favor of rehabilitation. This, however, only demonstrates that state narratives aren't monolithic. The dominant narrative of the state when I was incarcerated advocated for tough-on-crime policies, which included high mandatory minimum sentences, large budgets for police and prison guards, and zero tolerance for disobedience in grade schools. For people becoming disillusioned with the tough-on-crime approach, however, the state deployed the rehabilitation narrative. Both tough-on-crime and rehabilitation narratives serve to concentrate power and legitimacy in state prison systems. Both narratives justify the need for a state prison system, because whether you want to lock people up forever or provide them rehabilitation, you need the prison system. Within this framework, a person who thinks rehabilitation answers the problem of mass incarceration must collaborate with the perpetrators of mass incarceration—in a partnership where the perpetrators enjoy an extraordinary power differential—with the hope that they can resolve the problem together. This is like starting a nonprofit organization to combat domestic violence and then filling your board with unrepentant spouse abusers.

SQN awakened in me the knowledge that incarcerated people needed their own voice, their own power. It also drove home how impossible that goal was when the state itself was the gatekeeper of which incarcerated voices the public heard. When I co-founded Prison Renaissance, the baseline goal was that it would not be an organization that operates in partnership with prison administrators. Prison Renaissance was our version of power to the people. Because incarcerated people are not allowed to build power, our endeavor was dangerous. Every day, we lived in fear of being disappeared into solitary confinement. Incarcerated people in California aren't allowed to run businesses without the warden's permission, which we didn't have and would never get. Likewise, incarcerated people in California aren't allowed to be leaders, and if we become political, we risk hostility from a prison system that has an inordinate amount of control over whether we live or die. We have rights but very few means to enforce them, in either a court of law or a prison hearing. Even if we achieve our day in court—which often takes at least twelve months because of the Prison Litigation Reform Act—after the alleged violation, it's difficult to meet the legal requirements of a constitutional violation.

When I lived in High Desert State Prison, incarcerated people who'd reached the limit of the abuse they would take sometimes protested by covering their cell windows with paper. Guards require a clear view of every cell, so they can't ignore this form of protest. The guards' answer to this protest is to conduct a cell extraction, a process by which they forcibly remove the incarcerated person from the cell. It's also a process that requires approval from a higher-ranking officer. Which is why incarcerated people do it: it forces their complaints to be escalated to a supervisor. Between ten and twenty guards, equipped in riot gear, will conduct a cell extraction. The first thing they do when they enter a cellblock is to cover all the incarcerated people's windows so there are no witnesses to what happens. That way, if they violate the person's rights when extracting him, and he one day appears in court with a case against the officers, the only effective witnesses will be other correctional officers because incarcerated witnesses can't say, "I saw them violate his constitutional rights." They can't determine that excessive force was used by listening to the incident— only by seeing it—and while courts might frown at officers for covering all the windows, that's not a constitutional violation.

It is because of conditions like these that protect officers from accountability that I often characterize prisons as autocratic police states nestled in the shadow of American democracy. This is why co-founding Prison Renaissance was dangerous and why my co-founders and I lived in fear. We persisted, carefully, partly because it served our people and partly because it gave meaning to our traumas. In other words, as people deeply traumatized by prisons, we were afraid, but if we proved successful, we envisioned that other incarcerated people could live a little less afraid, a little less oppressed.

We also drew courage from two factors that afforded us a thin layer of protection. Two of us were writers, journalists, and organizers, so our careers attracted enough public prominence that we had relationships with influential people who would raise eyebrows if we disappeared. Second, our program activities were protected by the First Amendment; the prison couldn't stop us without risking a lawsuit. So it did what it is able to do with any program that relies on the prison system to exist: it pressured the leadership of *SQN* to stop us.

SQN began its campaign to stop Prison Renaissance under the guise of paternal concern. In our initial conversations, *SQN* leadership "worried" that I would get in trouble because I was essentially starting and running a business without approval from the warden. Wardens don't approve businesses in which the prison itself doesn't have a vested interest—one of the many ways prisons maintain a monopoly on incarcerated people's labor. I responded by telling *SQN* leadership I would assume that risk.

SQN escalated from using scare tactics under the guise of paternal concern to attacking my time (by trying to monopolize it), my access to word processors to produce my work, and my access to people in the free world. *SQN* leaders justified their attacks by saying they were concerned that the prison administration would wait for me to make a mistake, and once I stepped outside my legally protected rights, it would crush me and *SQN*, too, for being associated with me. To protect themselves from that, they had to scrutinize how I used my time during work hours, forbid me from working on any non-*SQN* project on the newsroom's computers, and restrict my access to volunteers and public forums. I welcomed the opportunity to build the resources for Prison Renaissance outside of state programs because that was, in fact, the point.

Prison Renaissance grew in visibility, and even though I agreed to all the conditions that *SQN* insisted on to keep the newspaper safe, conflict with *SQN* increased.

Conversations shifted from safety concerns to company loyalty. If I had extra time to build a company and brand for Prison Renaissance, why wasn't I putting that energy into increasing *SQN*'s success? When that tactic didn't work, *SQN* pressured me to hand over control of Prison Renaissance to the then editor in chief, who would then vet all its processes and allow me to run it as I saw fit at a later point. Surrendering control of Prison Renaissance to *SQN* was both tempting and unthinkable. It was tempting because a fairly common value among Black activists in my world at the time was that ownership of ideas doesn't matter—a practice of questionable value that deserves interrogation by another author. If ownership matters, then you've made it about you instead of your community. I felt shame, then, about wanting to retain ownership when surrendering the nonprofit might accomplish my ends more quickly and effectively.

But surrender was unthinkable because of what I'd observed about *SQN*. The paper perpetuated certain structural harms. As the voice of San Quentin State Prison, we wanted the world to believe that incarceration could be a benevolent experience wherein incarcerated people could listen to the rehabilitative wisdom of the state, fix themselves, and come back to society as productive citizens. The other side of that representation, of course, is that the incarcerated people who don't become productive citizens must not have listened and therefore need more incarceration until they do.

My peers and I were "special" because we were articulate, emotionally intelligent, accountable, remorseful; we contributed value to our prison community and to the communities we'd harmed before our arrests. We were acknowledged by prison guards, advocates, nonprofit executives, and senators as exemplars of change. We earned this acknowledgment through hard work, but our success could be weaponized to abandon all the incarcerated people who couldn't do exactly what we could do.

Our worthiness defined itself against the unworthiness of incarcerated people who didn't present like us. We "deserved" a second chance. They did not—at least not yet, not until they became more like my peers and me. This was the case despite the reality that the biggest difference between the so-called unworthy and the so-called worthy wasn't a moral one. The difference was that my peers and I had become fluent in the language of white capitalism, a language that signaled our commitment to upholding the power structure that released us from prison. We employed a politics of deference in a system that has to be challenged in order to change, and what we produced was the near enemy of empowerment for incarcerated people.

SQN did do some good in some people's lives. But what scared me about the prospect of *SQN* controlling Prison Renaissance was that the good that the newspaper accomplished relied on the support and goodwill of a single public information officer with a great deal of influence. I trusted this officer, who I won't name, to continue to support the good *SQN* did. I also respected him because he understood and supported what I was trying to do, and his influence was a key resource in my cold war to stay out of solitary confinement. But I knew that one day he would retire and someone else would fill his shoes. That someone would inherit the legitimacy machine we had made of *SQN*, and that person could use it to disseminate any message he or she wanted. That message would represent the voice of incarcerated leaders. The idea of surrendering Prison Renaissance to such a fate was indefensible.

So, I said no. Then, the editor in chief, who's an incarcerated person, sat me down and told me that if I didn't turn over control of Prison Renaissance to him, he would dedicate himself to destroying it and me. He held this threat over me the entire time he was in power, and when he stepped down as the head of the newsroom, his successor continued the persecution. From 2015 to 2019, the year I won my parole, building Prison Renaissance meant surviving a cold war with not only prison administrators but also the *San Quentin News*.

That this editor in chief, who ostensibly entered a profession to lift up the voice of the voiceless, came to persecute three incarcerated people who were fighting for the power, dignity, and voices of other incarcerated people illustrates the difference between building power and borrowing power. It takes power to change conditions, and what most prison programs do is borrow power from the system they're trying to fix in order to change it. To "fix" the prison system means different things to different people—abolish it, end its racist policy and practices, make it more humane, make it more effective at reducing recidivism. When people borrow power from oppressive systems to fix that system, they often are building bridges by convincing the oppressor that they have enough in common and can work together toward a short-term goal. For example, a program's executive begins talking with a prison administrator. The program executive wants to increase incarcerated people's rate of success after they leave prison. Let's say the executive is also an abolitionist who wants her program to have a dual purpose, as Prison Renaissance did. Her external brand is free college education for incarcerated people, but her internal goal is to use her college curricula as a medium to teach incarcerated leaders abolitionist strategy. She can't tell the administrator about her internal goal because the administrator wouldn't give her the power to achieve it. So, the executive proposes providing a college education for incarcerated people and exploits the administrator's desire for order by convincing him that a college education reduces disciplinary problems. The program executive wants to teach abolition; the prison administrator wants order; the bridge is the college program. Both parties agree to the program for different reasons, but they still cooperate to make it happen.

This is just a hypothetical example, not something I actually witnessed. I want to illustrate that if the bridge building convinces the administrator to green-light the college project, the executive will build the program, but the power to build is not hers. It's a loan from the prison. She will build a successful program, donors will dump money into it, then her family and co-workers will become dependent on the program, and she will ultimately become a hostage to her debt collectors. When the prison discovers she's teaching incarcerated people abolitionist strategy, they will tell her to stop, which she will do, or the prison will take back their power. When the prison says, "We want you to teach incarcerated people that prisons aren't so bad, that they're a place of opportunity," she will say "yes," or she will lose everything.

The editor in chief of *SQN* entered his profession to lift up the voice of the voiceless, but he built his vision with borrowed power. Then, prison administrators told him to stop Prison Renaissance or they would call in their loan. The *SQN* editor and everyone who relied on him faced the prospect of losing everything. He's human.

If we weigh it against the standard of building power, not borrowing it, Prison Renaissance wasn't a clear victory. We avoided borrowing power from the prison system—our power was ours—but we also had little power in comparison to other nonprofit organizations working with incarcerated people. We were an untried model developed and run by people without degrees, and funders prioritize organizations that align with the status quo. I'm still discovering how to build power effectively, but Prison Renaissance represents a moment of radical orientation on that journey.

Borrowing power from a white supremacist system ultimately strengthens the white power structure, so we charted a course toward building power instead of borrowing it, and the programs we created were steps toward that goal. That I don't yet know how to get to the place where I never have to borrow power from white supremacy is less important than the knowledge that we must get there to end white supremacy.

5

Police Identity Behind the Blue Wall

I invite you into some vision work. Imagine a world where no one is homeless. Imagine also that college is free, and the federal government pays off all the remaining college debt in the country. Would this be a better society? We could achieve this vision very quickly, as hundreds of scholars have already mapped the details of the plan. The material stumbling block our political leaders pretend they can't step over is the price tag. U.S. Senator Bernie Sanders's College for All Act would cost $48 billion a year, and the Education Data Initiative estimates that it would cost $800 billion over eleven years (or $73 billion a year) to make college free for everyone.[1] When we talk about homelessness, researchers don't agree on how much it would cost to end the crisis, but it ranges from $11 billion to $30 billion a year.[2] To remediate homelessness, solve the college debt crisis, and provide quality education would require a $151 billion-a-year spending commitment.

Now here's the billion-dollar question: Would you trade police and prisons for this society? According to the Urban Institute, we spent $222 billion on corrections and policing in 2022.[3] We could solve three of the largest social problems today by simply changing our spending habits. Perhaps you're thinking that would just trade one crisis for another. The argument might go as follows: crime is already a huge social problem, and without police and prisons, it would surely become our biggest crisis. That argument suffers from the imagination problem created by copaganda. "Copaganda" refers to U.S. police departments' manipulation of the news to create "a gap in public perception between what police actually do and what people think they do," a strategy on which they spend tens of millions of dollars annually.[4] It's how police departments sustain our imagination problem regarding public safety.

Given the pervasiveness of copaganda, people who believe we need police more than we need to end homelessness, college debt, and cost-prohibitive education can hardly be blamed. They're human, as subject to the psychology of effective branding as the rest of us when we buy a name-brand shoe. These people will believe that prisons protect us from having to encounter dangerous people and that police protect law-abiding citizens. But the public service narrative of police and prisons is another lie. The truth it conceals is that they protect the law-abiding citizens who support the police's agenda and intimidate (and some would say kill) the people who threaten their power. The lie conceals the actual identity and purpose of police and corrections. These institutions are not here to protect and serve us. Their function is to enforce and protect inequality. They do not work for us; they work for the white supremacist status quo established at the founding of this country.

When I was thirteen years old, everyone ran when the police drove up. We sold drugs, but that's not why everyone ran. We always carried water bottles, being sure never to hold more drugs on us than we could swallow in one gulp. One of the reasons we ran was love for each other. We knew that they couldn't chase us all, and although one or more of us would be caught, someone would escape police brutality that day. The biggest reason for running, however, was fear. The police made sure we were scared; that's part of the police ethos I've witnessed all my life—police talk about it in terms of respect. They made sure that we knew they could exercise total power over our lives. They made sure we felt subjugated—again, they call it respect. They threatened to and actually did plant drugs on us. They robbed us. They kidnapped us under color of law, dropped us off miles from home, and forced us to walk home through rival neighborhoods. And when they ran us to exhaustion and we surrendered, they'd gang up and kick us, children, into unconsciousness.

According to the personal accountability narrative, which functions to erase the state-sanctioned, routine child abuse I suffered, police abused me because I chose to live outside the law. I could've avoided it by staying in school and obeying my father. For many people, it's common sense that I would've avoided abuse by walking the straight and narrow, but this narrative is a tool of the police's public service lie. This fallacy makes us miss the structural patterns in my story that reveal the police's true identity.

In the summer of 2022, a Los Angeles deputy sheriff punched a mother in the face when she refused to let go of her infant.[5] That officer was pulled from duty only after another video surfaced showing another deputy tackling and pepper-spraying a woman because she filmed a man being handcuffed (the officers involved in that incident were also pulled from duty). When police killed Eric Garner in 2014, a bystander named Ramsey Orta recorded it, and the police retaliated.[6] Within twenty-four hours of the killing, the police pulled up at Orta's house, blasted his bedroom window with a spotlight while they menacingly stood outside their cars watching him. The day after the New York chief medical examiner officially ruled Eric Garner's death a homicide, police arrested Orta, mocking him by filming the arrest on camera phones. A few months later, police raided Orta's home, arrested him and his mother for drug sales, and then leveraged his mother's arrest to force him to plead guilty. A year later in prison, guards abused and tortured Orta, including what he believes was deliberate poisoning. In one instance, Orta's cell block suffered a lock-down which meant he could only eat what guards fed him. A guard beat him because Orta wouldn't eat the food that he suspected correctional officers had poisoned. While the guard beat him, the rest of the cellblock ate. They got sick, some vomiting blood, others convulsing on their floors. The guards laughed. No one was taken to the infirmary.

Again, some people might say Orta was incarcerated not as a result of police harassment but because he broke the law, or that the first woman was punched in the face because she obstructed the police in carrying out their duty. But few would argue that the woman filming the incident in LA should've been tackled for exercising her First Amendment right in a public space. However we feel about these events, it's hard to deny the patterns of police abuse that stretch from my childhood stories from the 1990s to a woman exercising her constitutional right in 2023.

The police want us to be afraid of them, they want us to believe they hold total power over our bodies, and they regularly reinforce this belief with extralegal violence. Their intimidation is a strategy; they're not seeking to intimidate just the mother who isn't compliant or the woman filming an arrest. They want you to be less likely to record them doing something extralegal, so that before you pull out your camera, you have to think about what will happen if you challenge their abuse. They want you to be scared, whether that means being so afraid of crime that you believe you need cops or so afraid of cops that you don't challenge their legitimacy. That's terrorism.

"Terrorism" is a big word, but the behavior of law enforcement professionals fits the definition. Title 18, Section 2331 of the United States Code defines terrorism as "activities that involve the use of violence or the threat of violence to intimidate or coerce a government, the civilian population, or any segment thereof, in furtherance of political or social objectives."

My friend is a political activist who organized in 2017 against the overfunding of the Alameda County Sheriff's Office. She's a person of color with no criminal record. In other words, she's made all the decisions required to be considered the good citizen whom we elect sheriffs to protect and serve. Her organizing objectives at the time were both political and social: to stop a jail expansion project and to push the county to audit the sheriff's spending habits, because she believed he was lying about his department's financial needs and it was resulting in the underfunding of social programs that healthy communities need. I can't define with certainty what the sheriff's political objectives are, but I can say that he is an elected leader who has political objectives, and those objectives apparently conflicted with my friend's political goals.

The sheriff's office intimidated my friend to further the sheriff's social and political goals. My friend believes that the sheriff's department retaliated against her for trying to hold the sheriff accountable. Unsurprisingly, in a world where law enforcement officers are themselves the gatekeepers and arbitrators of evidence, she can't prove the sheriff's office threatened her, but here are some facts: Within days of my friend making a media appearance or Alameda County making a decision related to the sheriff department's budget, my friend consistently would be targeted for harassment. Someone smashed her car window outside her home and left a note on a brick: "We know where you live, watch out." Her laptop, which contained her calendars and documents about her organizing, was stolen. While she was out of town on vacation, someone totaled her car, which was parked in an upscale neighborhood in Oakland. By "totaled," I mean they rammed a vehicle into the back of her car. Then, they backed up and rammed the side of her car. Then, they rammed the front of her car. Before they left, they smashed her window and left a note tucked in her car's sun visor. She found it days later when it dropped in her lap. It read, "Fuck you [my friend's name]. Welcome back." After this last incident, my friend intentionally decided not to do as many interviews with reporters as before, nor let people she supervised take her place in the interviews. Today, when presented with media opportunities she still thinks about the threat of retaliation and I assume she very likely turns many down in order to feel safer.

On April 4, 2015, Feidin Santana similarly feared retaliation after filming a North Charleston, South Carolina, police officer carefully line up his sights, take a breath, and fire eight rounds at Walter Scott, an unarmed Black man running in the opposite direction. The officer then dropped his Taser next to Scott to support a cover-up story that Scott took the Taser in a tussle with the officer. Santana reported that he initially held on to the video because he knew what had happened after Orta filmed Eric Garner's death.[7]

What my friend who now avoids media interviews and people afraid to film police have experienced constitutes intimidation to achieve political or social aims. That's terrorism.

It's a national problem. In Mississippi, six deputy sheriffs broke into the home of two Black men. The deputies were known for regularly using excessive force and even celebrated it by calling themselves the "Goon Squad." They handcuffed, kicked, waterboarded, and attempted to sexually assault the men while screaming racial slurs for nearly two hours.[8] Then, one of the sheriffs shoved his gun into the mouth of one of the victims and shot him. (Miraculously, the victim survived.) Why did the deputies do this? According to news reports, one of the deputy's neighbors called him personally—not 911— with a complaint that two Black men were living with a white woman next door and that the Black men were behaving suspiciously. According to anyone paying attention to American history, the Goon Squad hurt these men because they were Black men living with a white woman. That's terrorism.

These deputies felt justified committing fifteen felonies—to "protect and serve" what? It appears that they were protecting white supremacy, but people dismiss such incidents as a matter of bad apples ruining the reputation of good cops. To be clear, this analogy doesn't hold up to scrutiny: bad apples actually do spoil the whole barrel. We wouldn't approach a barrel full of rotten apples and eat one of them, telling ourselves it's not the apple's fault that a different apple made it rotten. We'd get rid of the barrel. The use of the term "bad apple," however, has shifted—especially as it's used for police. It's come to mean that we shouldn't see a few bad apples as representative of a group. If we leave behind the apple metaphor and simply say we shouldn't allow a few harmful people to define a group's character, I agree. It acknowledges that within any social group, we'll find people who serve a greater purpose than themselves, people who are just living their lives, and people who commit tremendous harms. In the case of police, though, you've missed the problem if you're talking about it in terms of bad versus good actors, because the crisis isn't rotten people. The crisis is a rotten institution.

In 2023, a training officer in Texas, Jonathan Macheca, texted a picture of a swastika and lightning bolts to his trainees—arguably, the next generation of Goon Squads.[9]

Macheca accidentally sent the text to a civilian, who presumably went to the media with it. The subsequent news headline was that two officers were fired, but I would argue they were fired only because their harm was exposed. Macheca's LinkedIn profile says he worked for the Southlake PD as "Master Peace Officer" for fifteen years.[10] He worked for a small police force of sixty-seven for fifteen years.[11] Anyone who lives in a small town can tell you it is extremely unlikely that other officers didn't know Macheca was a white supremacist, yet not one story has surfaced of a "good officer" coming forward; not one trainee saw a problem with the swastikas and reported him. Or if they reported him, the superior who received the report covered it up, just as the Goon Squad tried to cover up their felonious torture of two men.

What we witnessed with Macheca, what we witness with all the disciplinary actions against police misconduct, is an individual response to a structural problem. I can imagine a campaign arising on the left to ensure the removal of all racist trainers, maybe even requiring a moral litmus test for future trainers, but that misses the point. Bad officers aren't creating the culture; police culture attracts and then empowers bad officers. Even if we invested billions in officer retraining and officer accountability initiatives, how would we even know the strategy rooted out the so-called bad apples? The police wouldn't tell us. They haven't been telling us. Such dishonesty and loyalty, commonly referred to as the "Blue Wall of Silence," is endemic to police procedure. In a 2021 article, civil rights attorney James Mueller noted that since 1988, he's "never, ever" seen a deputy or a police office report another officer for excessive force.[12] This form of corruption, one of many in policing, is an institutional problem, not a problem of bad apples.

Here's the humbling and scary truth I've learned: because of the power disparity that police have built over decades between them and regular citizens, everyday people don't have the power to implement structural change within police departments. One reason is police unions. Unions use collective bargaining to fight for the interests of their workers, and in the police field, you can tell where those interests lie when you set the history of police union victories alongside the statistics on police abuse. Professor Rob Gillezeau did just that and found a correlation between police unions' influence and a substantial rise in police killings of Black people. As Gillezeau explained, "Collective bargaining rights are being used to protect the ability of officers to discriminate in the disproportionate use of force against the non-white population."[13] He isn't alone in his findings.[14]

Again, the police deploy terrorism to protect and serve white supremacy, and their unions fight to preserve their capacity to lawfully do so.

The U.S. has always used police as guardians of white supremacy. The first police forces were slave patrols in the

1700s that crushed uprisings and captured escaped slaves.[15] One hundred years later, Northern cities established police forces, and these forces became best known for crushing labor strikes.[16] The throughline in the origins of the police in the South and North is that in both regions, police forces were formed in response to citizens resisting white power structures. This is an important pattern to recognize when analyzing police unions' rise to power.

Initially, police were denied collective-bargaining rights by states and union federations for reasons ranging from conflict of interest to public safety.[17] Decision makers changed their minds in the 1960s, which notably coincided with the rise of the civil rights movement. In other words, because citizens were revolting against the white power structure, states needed to suppress what they saw as unrest, so they conceded police the right to unionize. These unions have since become a powerful force in politics, spending hundreds of millions to influence elections and public policy.[18]

The apparatus for changing the policing institution is policy, and the $135 billion that taxpayers invested in police in 2012, for example, translates to more police union power, which in turn translates to lobbyists with the power to block meaningful change through policy.[19] This would be a crisis on its own, but support for police extends beyond their unions and lobbyists. Police have the support of racist senators, organizations, and philanthropists. This dilemma illustrates for me the failure of our democracy, because citizens have become hostages to police power.

We can't turn to our mayors or city councils, because police unions have a stranglehold on electoral politics. In 2020, council members in Santa Ana, California, tried to divert police funds to community-building projects and back a police chief committed to police accountability. The police union responded by spending more than $400 million to install two council members and oust the police chief.[20] Two years later, the union consolidated its power over the city council by adding two more pro–police union members. The union-controlled council voted for raises for the police and hired fifty more officers.[21] In 2022, Sarena Townsend, the head of internal intelligence in New York jails, angered the corrections officers' union when she cracked down on excessive force in jails. The mayor, who had close ties with a lobbying firm working for the union, appointed a new jail commissioner, who fired her.[22] When the City of Minneapolis tried to defund the police in the wake of George Floyd's death, they applied for federal funding to reduce crime and opioid-related overdoses.[23] Not only did Minneapolis meet the eligibility requirements for the grant, but in the scoring system used by the federal agency, they ranked second highest out of 212 applicants.[24] The federal agency refused to grant the funds, writing in a report that Defund the Police advocacy would prevent the proper administration of the funds.[25]

Police terrorism holds our public officials hostage just as it holds citizens hostage. It seems to me that the only people who can change the police are the police themselves. It's not reasonable to expect them to transform themselves into public servants, because, by design, that mission doesn't align with their founding principles and the power structures that have been created for them.

We have only to examine the last fifty years of police history to see that they're committed to terrorism. During that period, secret cadres developed in police and sheriff departments. These cadres identify themselves with tattoos, hand signs, and rituals that valorize both excessive force and falsifying police reports. For anyone else, these acts would constitute criminal conspiracy; for police forces, it's often just deemed unconstitutional (and unreasonably hard to prove).

Los Angeles created the Civilian Oversight Commission in 2016 to monitor the LA County Sheriff's Department. In 2023, a seventy-page report by the commission found that not only had racist sheriff gangs with names like the Executioners, the Banditos, and the Regulators been operating in Los Angeles for at least fifty years, but these "sheriff gangs control many of LA County's patrol stations as opposed to the station sergeants and captains."[26] Sheriff Robert Luna, newly elected in

2022 on a promise to bring "new accountability and leadership" to the sheriff's department, acknowledged the existence of these gangs and vowed "there will be absolutely no tolerance for deputy gangs." He repeated similar rhetoric to the sheriffs who had protected and proliferated the deputy gangs for fifty years. This only confirmed a long-standing pattern: law enforcement will say and do anything to protect its brand of public service in order to mask its true identity as a terrorist institution ultimately deployed in our country to preserve white supremacy.

The first major stories about deputy gangs in Los Angeles broke in 1991, when a federal judge found that a neo-Nazi, white supremacist gang that called itself the Vikings had routinely violated civil rights and used terrorist-like tactics with the knowledge of the county sheriff's department.[27] One article that covered a week in the life of these sheriff gangs illustrated just a small sample of their harms. On February 11, 1990, deputies slammed a Latino man's head against their squad car window until the window cracked. On the same day, two blocks away, deputies dragged two men off their front porch, beat their heads with flashlights, and left them in the streets. A neighbor called the sheriff's department to complain about the brutality. The deputies returned and drove the beaten men to the hospital, where they were arrested. No medical treatment. Four days later, ten deputies ransacked a shop, threatened two men with guns, and beat them. This is just one week representing week after week of police terror in Los Angeles County.[28]

The sheriff at the time of the federal case, Sherman Block, insisted that the Vikings were just a harmless social group—a sports club. The sheriff's department had many such groups (many of which would later be revealed to be sheriff gangs), and Block's administration fought the court tooth and nail to block the judge's injunction. What was that injunction? The two primary requirements were that the sheriff's department abide by its own policies regarding use of force and searches, and that it send the judge every brutality complaint lodged against it. This may seem like a different response than Sheriff Luna's thirty-one years later. A pattern unites them: upon a closer look at both Block's and his successors' response, a clear strategy emerges.

For decades, Black philosophers and activists have described the police as a colonizing force. Frantz Fanon, a psychiatrist and anti-colonial theorist born in 1925 on the Caribbean island of Martinique, is one such philosopher. His insights on predictable cycles between colonizers and those who resist them illuminate the patterns that unite the public responses of Sheriff Luna and Sheriff Block to sheriff gangs. He noted that when revolt happens in a colony, police forces are instructed to modify their behavior to put on a nicer face and offer "paltry measures and clever window dressing" designed to defuse the community outrage at the heart of revolution.[29] In the case of the LA County Sheriff's Department, window dressing manifests as public declarations that the department supports people of color and won't tolerate the "bad apple" deputies. It manifests as promises about change that are never followed by substantial action addressing the essence of the problem. These smiling-face tactics give the people who are suffering a feeling that things are changing, and white supremacist forces exploit this.[30]

In Fanon's analysis, people who've experienced prolonged oppression from the state have grown so accustomed to contempt and brutality that any degree of relief threatens to sweep them away with blinding elation—blinding, because they don't see that it's not change; it's a near enemy. For example, when a sheriff fires a deputy for misconduct in the community (a rare occurrence) or when the larger institution of criminal justice sacrifices one of the thousands of cops who have been killing Black and Brown people for decades to a jury trial, that doesn't happen because the sheriff or the institution has suddenly awakened to the light of justice. That light has always been clear, and acting upon it has always been an option. What has shifted is the sheriff's or the institution's assessment of what it will take to continue growing power. In other words, institutions of white supremacy and their agents, when faced with resistance to injustices, will concede and do *only* what they think they must to maintain the status quo. Nothing more.

This pattern of concessions and the power-holding motives behind them is what unites law enforcement's varied responses to community abuse, from Sheriff Block to Sheriff Luna—and from California to Texas to New York. Here's how the pattern played out in Los Angeles.

The federal judge in 1991 found that racist deputy gangs—in particular, a gang called the Vikings—employed terrorist-like tactics to routinely violate civil rights, and did so with the tacit support of the sheriff's department. Private investigator David Lynn's testimony in this case, delivered before both the California Senate and the U.S. Commission on Civil Rights, adds texture to what the judge meant by "tacit support." In an article for the *Press-Telegram*, he described an institutionalized culture wherein deputies viewed Black and Brown communities as expendable and, acting on this disregard, they routinely committed malicious acts against people of color.[31] These deputies did so knowing that prosecutors would turn a blind eye, and that any awards from civil lawsuits won against them would be paid by taxpayers. What is more, they knew they had their superiors' approval of their actions and would suffer no consequences for abuse, torture, and murder (so long as they were perceived as harming the right people).

The right people to victimize included officers who obstructed the political aims of deputy gangs. One Viking, Kathy Kay, reported her lieutenant's personal car as stolen along with a warning that her lieutenant was armed and dangerous—Kay was acquitted in a jury trial of any wrongdoing. According to this same lieutenant, Vikings intimidated officers regularly.[32] The command staff tasked with holding racist deputies accountable would receive Valentine's cards with dead rats inside, suffer car drivers' attempts to run them down, and have hearses dispatched to their private residences at three in the morning. A Black sergeant received a loaded gun in the mail rigged to fire when he opened the package. This same sergeant later got a Vikings tattoo, presumably joining the monster to avoid being devoured by it—get with it, or get run over by it.

This history shows us that law enforcement has no collective desire to change its stripes. The officers at the top of the command chain that ought to be tasked with revolutionizing the status quo are as afraid to challenge the racist structures of their institution as my activist friend—as bystanders with cameras, as mayors, as council members—for fear that the sheriff's office will one day retaliate. Leaders in law enforcement are so mired in this cycle of terrorism that a Black sergeant joined a neo-Nazi deputy gang to survive.

Block and his administration denied the existence of gangs, claiming the Vikings were a harmless social club. The department attacked the Vikings' victims, claiming they were lying criminals, and Block went as far as to suggest that gang members (implicitly Black and Brown) were banding together to discredit deputies.[33] Despite the clear existence of sheriff gangs, Block didn't have to concede or admit anything to maintain law enforcement's status quo. So, he didn't. And whether he did so out of the same terror that coerced a Black sergeant to join the Vikings or did so out of malicious complicity is irrelevant to the intractability of the police problem in the United States.

One year after Block's denial, special counsel James Kolts, appointed by the Department of Justice (DOJ), released a 359-page report following an investigation of the sheriff's department, concluding that "although there is some evidence suggestive of the existence of deputy gangs, such evidence is, at most, inconclusive."[34] The report did cite an alarming number of excessive force complaints against Lynwood station—the Viking's homebase—as well as racialized hiring practices. After the DOJ-initiated investigation made a legal fact of racialized hiring practices and excessive force complaints in the sheriff's office, Block had to admit they were problems. Five years later, he told the U.S. Commission on Civil Rights that he'd made huge strides to reduce use of force by deputies, track problem officers, and sensitize staff to different cultures. He continued to characterize claims related to organized sheriff gangs in his department as ridiculous.[35] It's debatable whether he'd made great strides or he offered window dressing, but regardless, we can see that familiar pattern of admitting to what is required in order to maintain legitimacy, and nothing else.

It's clear that these gangs were a problem in 1991, because twenty years later, Sheriff Robert Luna finally acknowledged them. Block's denials might tempt some to shake their heads and deride him for being out of touch or not wanting to know, but such sentiments fail to recognize that before Block became the sheriff, he was a deputy for twenty-six years who began his career in the lower ranks.[36] He came up in the culture that produced racist deputy gangs, and whether or not he joined one, he can't both be politically savvy enough to rise to sheriff and too stupid to know that groups of racist deputies were terrorizing communities of color with impunity. Of course, he knew and bullshitted us about it, but even that's beside the point. It's beside the point because his abetment (and that of the sheriffs after him) isn't about him; it's about us, a public nurtured on white hegemony, and it's about what needs to shift in the ways we think about and see both law enforcement and its relationship to white supremacy.

Today, too many people hear about the deputy gangs, hear the long line of denials by sheriff departments, and they fall for the traps built around their imaginations. They blame leadership. The general sentiment ranges from contempt to shoulder shrugs. Perhaps we indict a particular leader for incompetence or corruption; rarely do mainstream conversations indict the institution, the soil, that the leader grew from. Rarely do we examine whether leaders in law enforcement are in fact competently performing a nationwide-sanctioned role to preserve white supremacy—the very role with which the earliest police in the U.S. were tasked. It's another version of the "bad apple" thinking. We're encouraged to shift blame from the structure to the individual, and we're ignoring the logic behind how leader after leader who takes the helm becomes another bad apple.

We sometimes say that deputy gangs are a cancer, but the acknowledgment misidentifies the problem by missing the point of what cancer is. Cancer is a process; the tumors that kill us are a product of that process. Similarly, deputy gangs are a product of a process, white supremacy. Understanding that makes it easier to see why we must replace policing with a community-based institution vested in safety for all members. It's why we must get serious about a national strategy to abolish the police, because cancer untreated only gets worse until it kills us. The policing institution itself is a product of the same cancerous process giving rise to and investing an inordinate amount of power in deputy gangs, which is why we see the same patterns playing out in law enforcement across the country.

Since 2000, investigators have uncovered law enforcement officers with connections to white supremacist groups in states including Alabama, California, Connecticut, Florida, Illinois, Louisiana, Michigan, Nebraska, Oklahoma, Oregon, Texas, Virginia, Washington, and West Virginia.[37] The problem is so bad that the FBI warns its agents investigating domestic terrorism that white "supremacist and anti-government militia groups they investigate often have 'active links' to law enforcement officials." Examples abound. In 2020, three Wilmington, North Carolina, police officers were caught on camera using racial epithets, criticizing a magistrate and the police chief in racist terms, and talking about shooting Black people—including a Black police officer.

In 2001, two Texas sheriff's deputies were exposed recruiting other officers to the KKK.[38] In 2005, an internal investigation revealed that a Nebraska state trooper was participating in a members-only KKK chat room. In 2015, a Louisiana police officer was photographed giving a Nazi salute at a Klan rally. In 2019, reports revealed a Michigan police officer with a framed KKK application in his home. In Salem, Oregon, a video recording showed a police officer asking heavily armed white men dressed in militia clothing to step inside a building while the police arrested protesters for failing to comply with curfew orders.[39]

Some officers lost their jobs in these cases, but many of them simply use their networks to get jobs in other police departments. In 2017, the police chief in Colbert, Oklahoma, resigned after he was outed as a neo-Nazi, and the neighboring Oklahoma police department hired him the following year.[40] In 2018, the Greensboro, Maryland, police chief was charged with falsifying records to hire a police officer who had previously been forced to resign from the Dover, Delaware, police department after he kicked a Black man in the face and broke his jaw.[41] It's tempting for some to look at the geography of these incidents and dismiss race and policing as a Southern, Middle America, conservative Republican sin. It's not. In blue, liberal Connecticut, state troopers forged sixth thousand traffic citations to white people to cover up the racial profiling of people of color.[42] These are only cases that have gone public. For each one journalists uncover, there are thousands more incidents that law enforcement has covered up.

What we see accompanying these patterns of racist cops terrorizing and killing but failing to be held accountable is the same performative strategy employed by the Los Angeles County Sheriff's Department. They admitted and conceded only what they had to in order to maintain public legitimacy while doubling down on perpetuating the brand and influence of an illegitimate law enforcement apparatus.

After Sheriff Block, Lee Baca came to power. In 1998, journalists wrote about yet more deputy gangs in Los Angeles that had been growing in power since 1971: the Cavemen, the Grim Reapers, the Rattlesnakes.[43] What was Baca's response? He criticized the deputy gangs for their tattoos because the tattoos were unprofessional and undermined public trust in the sheriff department. Eventually, in 2005, he required deputies to cover their tattoos while on duty. He told the public that he sent a no-nonsense Latino commander to run the station that had served as headquarters for the Vikings. He suggested that when he'd been the department chief addressing the problem of deputy gangs, his hands had been tied, but now that he was sheriff, he could take bolder action.[44] The so-called bolder action he took: he promoted Paul Tanaka, a known member of the Vikings, to be his second-in-command.

Sheriff Alex Villanueva served as sheriff between 2018 and 2022. He revived Block's narrative by denying that deputy gangs had ever existed, but an investigative report released in 2023 by the Sheriff Oversight Commission found that Villanueva's department "at minimum tolerated, if not rewarded" deputy gangs.[45] It would be more accurate to say he protected the deputy gangs.

In September 2018, sometime after midnight four members of a sheriff gang known as the Banditos showed up to a department party at Kennedy Hall in East Los Angeles and in the parking lot assaulted four deputies who refused to support the Banditos' illicit activities. Two deputies were beaten unconscious. Dozens of deputies stood around watching the crime happen. Some cheered. After these severe beatings, one of the assailants, Rafael Munoz, reportedly bragged that Sheriff Villanueva would make sure no Bandito was prosecuted for a crime dozens of deputies witnessed.[46] This is the police's true identity.

Munoz was fired. Then Villanueva rehired him.[47] Munoz was one of four hundred fired law enforcement officers that Villanueva fought to get rehired. Villanueva also rehired Caren Carl Mandoyan, a member of a deputy gang called the Grim Reapers. Mandoyan had been fired for stalking, harassment, and abuse of another deputy. Not only did the sheriff rehire Mandoyan, Villanueva gave him $200,000 in backpay.[48]

The sheriff as of 2024, Robert Luna, is the new apple tree in the same soil. He acknowledges deputy gangs exist and says he won't tolerate them. Same story. He concedes only that which he calculates he must in order to maintain the facade of police legitimacy.

Luna took the same approach when he was the chief of the worst-ranking police department in California in terms of accountability, systemic racism, and police brutality: the Long Beach Police Department (LBPD).[49] In 2018, days before a statewide transparency law would open certain police misconduct records for the first time, LBPD destroyed twenty-three years of records. The administrators at Luna's department claimed they needed to clear storage space.[50] They lied because they didn't think they had to admit what they were doing. Internal emails later revealed that Luna had circulated messages from outside attorneys advising the department to purge records in order to avoid the new law. In the same year, scandal rocked the LBPD because Luna and his department conducted police business using a self-deleting messaging app to ensure their conversations wouldn't be discoverable.[51] Only after news coverage exposed Luna did he discontinue the department-wide practice.

This is who the police are, a state-sanctioned terrorist institution with public service branding. We see the shape of terrorism in so many different contexts—from police kicking children to intimidating concerned citizens. Why do we struggle to confront this reality and abandon this rotten institution?

I'm often leading conversations about the police problem, and inevitably someone will say some version of "But we need the police." If we don't have police, who do we turn to when we are harmed? The concern is human. Underlying it are the same human concerns that abolitionists hold: we share the goal of safe neighborhoods; we acknowledge the challenge of people who commit harm in communities. What abolitionists have realized is that we don't need the police; "need" is a misnomer.

We're *dependent* on the police, and a huge difference exists between needing someone and being dependent on them. We wouldn't tell an abused wife in a co-dependent relationship that they need their spouse. If the wife faced limited opportunities for work, childcare, mental health care, and housing, we would understand that she may not have the right circumstances to exit, but we would never say she needs that abusive relationship. Instead, we'd start to think about how to bridge the wife's dire situation with a new set of circumstances that does empower her to leave. That's what abolitionists are trying to do—create new systems and ways of thinking that provide us a bridge to a world where we're no longer dependent on police. Those entrenched in law enforcement fight abolitionists tooth and nail, just as abusive husbands battle any attempts to break their hold on their spouses.

We're in a co-dependent relationship with an immoral, violent institution. Police dominate and control us using the same tactics that violently abusive spouses use to maintain power and control. For example, withholding (affection and finances) is a common tactic of abusers. From Oakland to New York City, when communities talk about reducing funding for the police, a common tactic arises from police departments: withhold service.[52] They maliciously slow down their response times and refuse to answer non-emergency calls to exacerbate crises and desperation. Their goal is to abuse communities into believing that they need more police.

Police also withhold finances to foster dependency on them. Cities don't propose budget cuts to police forces for spite or for kicks. They propose cuts often to divert funds to services, such as education, restorative justice, and housing, that communities say they need more than oversized police forces. It's a democratic process that police undermine by intimidating council members. They're siphoning the resources needed to build the bridge from our dependence on them to a world where we can be safe without them.

Abusers minimize and deny blame, and we see plenty of that not only in the Los Angeles County Sheriff Department's handling of sheriff gangs but in law enforcement's response to police brutality nationwide. Police regularly threaten harm both with words and through their reactions when we resist their control (not only when we break the law but also when we aren't doing what they want us to do). We see this in their handling of nonviolent civil protest or when they intimidate bystanders recording their abuses on smartphones. Police even threaten you when you are doing what they want—in a traffic stop, for example, standing at your car window with their hand on their gun. Public intimidation (of the general public, not just so-called criminals) is an inseparable part of the police's social fabric. If you doubt that, I ask you to run a thought exercise: Imagine two police officers at 1 a.m. in a badly lit alley. Picture yourself approaching them. Take a moment to imagine the weather. Is it cold? What are you wearing? What do the police look like? Were they talking or silent when you approached? Hold this vision in your head. Now, with no witnesses or cameras to record what happens next, imagine saying, "I fucking hate pigs." What do you think would happen next? More importantly, when you imagined saying "I fucking hate pigs," what did you feel in your body? If you felt any signs of threat, why? Run the same thought exercise, but instead of police officers, imagine a teacher ("I hate teachers") or even a judge. It would be ill-advised to do this in all instances, but most people would see the serious peril in doing this with police. Because the police intimidate us.

What unites police and abusers in domestic violence cycles is the prior use of violence. A husband who tells his spouse, "Just shut up," is an asshole. Perhaps his spouse will respond, "Fuck you, *you* shut up." But it's another beast if that husband has previously committed violence against his spouse and she tells him to shut up. The spouse must now think about the violent consequences that may follow her response. Just as my friend who organized against the Alameda County Sheriff's Office must think about the consequences of accepting a media appearance. Just as the woman in Los Angeles whom cops pepper-sprayed for exercising her First Amendment right must think twice before videotaping police misconduct again. Just as the command staff in the Los Angeles County Sheriff's Department must find ways to be in support of sheriff gangs, whether they want to or not.

The other truth I think people are loath to admit: our denial is a coping mechanism to deal with the police's pervasive intimidation. I see this often in community conversations about criminal justice that I facilitate. In one, a person that I'll call Malik recalled a moment when he called the police on a mentally ill, unhoused man. The unhoused man had held Malik's porch hostage for three hours, which scared Malik. When the police arrived two hours later, they handled the situation with care, according to Malik. They gave the unhoused man his space and called in a non-police mental health team who resolved the situation. Malik was visibly uncomfortable telling this story, perhaps a little defensive given that a lot of respected people in the room were police abolitionists who believed calling the police on a mentally ill person is a well-known way to get that person shot to death. The point Malik said he wanted to make was that, yes, awful police existed, but he had to believe that 95 percent of them were upstanding people doing noble jobs. In other words, on balance, having our modern police force is overwhelmingly good for most of society. Malik kept using phrases like "We have to believe" and "I hope."

Given how vulnerable it can feel to share personal stories, I didn't point out how often he used these phrases—though I wanted to. I wanted to ask him, why did we have to believe that the horrible things we know about violent cops is a story about bad apples and not a story about an institutional staple? I think the answer is that the reality is a nightmare that can easily make us feel small. White hegemony has infused in us a sense of powerlessness that necessitates us feeling small should we face this nightmare. Not only has this hegemony always led with "public good" narratives at odds with the realities we see, but, from Belgium's King Leopold killing millions of Congolese in the late nineteenth century to the FBI destroying Black leaders and organizations in the U.S., the powers who've built their hegemony on our backs have consistently destroyed anyone who challenged their narratives. That's terrifying.

But we are not small. We have but to expose and shed the limited imaginations we've inherited to begin the journey of becoming free.

6

A Vision of Abolition

W hat does a world where we don't put people in prison for breaking the law look like, and how do we get there? I've had a lot of conversations about this. In general, people resonate with adopting a more humane approach to drug use, property crimes, and mental health issues so long as they also feel that the approach is effective. The question people struggle with is, what do we do when someone commits a violent act? We have to collectively answer this question through innovation and community consensus, but a signature guiding principle of an abolitionist future is that we strive to respond to violence in a way that transforms situations of unsafety to social conditions that support more safety. It's the inverse of what we have with our current punitive legal system, whose approach I characterize as two steps forward, four steps back.

In our current system, a person commits harm, and their incarceration makes the person harmed feel safer. More accurately, they've been taught to believe they're safer if we lock up the person who harmed them; in reality, they often continue to feel unsafe long after a judge sentences their assailant. They are living the reality of what the crisis of mass incarceration has taught us: our carceral machine makes society less safe.

Sociologists and activists have long studied and documented prison's criminogenic effects, how prisons translate to high rates of domestic violence and suicide among correctional officers, and how prisons become black holes for tax dollars that we could otherwise use to become safer by addressing issues like poverty, mental wellness, housing, and education. In other words, some people experience a forward momentum toward safety when police arrest "the bad guy" (two steps forward), but then we look up years later and find ourselves in a world suffering a more desperate state (four steps back).

I characterize the abolition vision—responses to harm that transmute situations of unsafety to social conditions that support more safety—as two steps back, four steps forward because although communities will still suffer setback by harms committed within them, they will ultimately find themselves living in a safer and stronger society. Not only will the harms against them be remediated, but the conditions that led to the harm will be transformed so that there are now significantly fewer committed.

Today, our legal system does almost nothing to remediate the harm caused by violent crime, and the zero-sum analysis I used in chapter 4 for the interventions of nonprofit organizations illustrates why. To refresh your memory, this zero-sum analysis takes a situation involving multiple stakeholder groups; measures the distribution of power among the groups (represented by a

10-point system); introduces an intervention—in this scenario, a case in our current legal system—and then remeasures the distribution of power to determine the impact of the intervention on stakeholders. In our criminal legal system, the primary stakeholders are generally recognized as the state (along with its municipal representatives), the community wherein the harm occurred, the individual who committed the harm, and the person harmed. I've assigned the state 4 points, the community wherein the harm occurred, 3 points; the individual who harmed, 1.5 points; and the person harmed, 1.5 points. Again, it's not important to determine exactly how much power each stakeholder has; the assignments only need to communicate which stakeholders have more power than others. This exercise isn't used to understand how much each party has; its purpose is to measure the redistribution of power between stakeholders to see who benefits most after the legal intervention.

Let's practice this analysis using fictional characters. James robs a woman named Pelia—move 1 point from Pelia to James because Pelia's loss of money and safety represents a loss of power. The community's loss in safety represents a similar loss—move 1 point from the community to James. Pelia wants to regain some sense of power, so she calls the police. The police arrest James and take most of his power, which accrues to the state. Now, the state has 7 points; the community has 2; James and Pelia have 0.5 each.

What does the state do with the power it's taken from James, some of which rightly belongs to Pelia and the community? Does Pelia or the community have any real say in what happens to James next? No, not unless they ask for what the state already committed to giving: punishment and imprisonment. The state in these cases operates from a paternal standpoint, following a process that disempowers every party except the state. The state's representative, the county, puts James on trial; after it gets the testimony it wants from the person harmed, it essentially tells Pelia, "Okay, great; now, go back to your job." After the trial, Pelia's support (if she gets any) will likely come from members of her community. Such support, whether financial or emotional, is a resource, so the community loses a point in order for her to regain power she lost. The person who harmed her and her community is incarcerated now, so perhaps she feels safer. That too is a form of power we can add to her pool of points.

We might think that this feeling of safety should accrue also to her community's pool, but according to the rules of using this tool, we can't assign power to a stakeholder without identifying who experiences the corresponding loss. The pools available to feed into the community are Pelia's, James's, and the state's. When a point accrues to Pelia, it doesn't come from the state, because the state isn't actually giving her or the community anything. The state delivers a narrative that manipulates

Pelia and her community into believing they're more safe, that justice has been served, but the conditions that led to James harming Pelia remain unchanged. The world Pelia lives in hasn't become safer. This is the logic of manipulation driving the system—the state uses other people's power to its own ends. So, in this case, it is James who loses power to give Pelia the illusion of safety, which means he gives up the last 0.5 point he has. I could have used a larger pool of points to ensure he doesn't run out, but the logic of manipulation ensures that the state would still take James's power and keep the power that belonged to Pelia and the community for itself.

If we repeat this process over and over, the distribution of points may change (e.g., the community could take its power at the victim's expense), but in each case, the state will grow in power and the society the state claims to serve will lose power.[1] This creates a cycle of dependence on a system that isn't working for the people it ostensibly serves.

Back to the controlling questions: What does a world where we don't put people in prison look like, and how will we remediate harm while tending to the conditions primarily responsible for harm?

Let's tell a different story of James and Pelia, this one set in an abolitionist world. (Trigger warning: this story involves sexual violence.) In this story, James doesn't rob Pelia, because property crimes are exceedingly rare in a society where everyone has housing and sufficient income. He rapes her. After one of the deepest violations a person can experience, Pelia doesn't call the police. She can't. The last police station was closed five years ago as part of a ten-year project to phase out modern law enforcement. During this phaseout period, legislators diverted half of the $209 billion a year we had spent on police and incarceration into a transformative justice economy. One component of this economy consists of community-based organizations that have formed coalitions of peacekeepers. Because these peacekeepers are now the first responders to violence, Pelia reports her rape to them.

The peacekeepers take Pelia's statement and enroll her in the state-funded harm recovery program. In this program, Pelia has the option of receiving a $30,000 stipend, in addition to subsidies for housing expenses, to take leave from work and focus for the next year on healing from the trauma of rape. Another part of our transformative justice infrastructure is what are called Healing Cities. They are actually not cities but townships developed through land trusts during the ten-year phaseout of modern law enforcement, and there are two kinds: towns designed for survivors like Pelia and towns dedicated to people like James who've committed harm. Somatic healers, circle keepers, body workers, therapists, ancestral culture keepers, sexologists, fire keepers, and earth shamans serve as facilitators in the cities, helping to heal the ruptures that inevitably happen in communities. Pelia has the option to spend any part of her one-year leave at a Healing City.

While Pelia is giving her statement, another group of peace-keepers conduct an investigation to verify James's violation and find him. James lives in a neighboring city, so they contact his local peacekeepers, who knock on James's door during dinner. Most peacekeepers work in the communities in which they grew up, so one of the three that shows up on James's doorstep is a friend from high school days. Another became friends with James through the regular community events peacekeepers hold.

James opens the door, sees the peacekeepers and drops his eyes, unable to look at his old friend. "Come in," he mumbles and retreats to a dinner table in his kitchen.

For those who consider it unlikely that someone who knows they've been caught breaking the law would react this way, I'd like to share a little-known reality of how peace is kept in prison. As often as not, it's kept through the relationships between friends. When a violation occurs in prison, often the aggrieved parties approach the violator's affinity group. Someone within that group will consult with the violator's inner circle. Someone in that inner circle will talk to him, hear him, and say when appropriate, "You are wrong, make it right." This works as well as it does because humans are social beings. We need each other, and the thought of losing our connection to the people we love, the people who respect us, can be as powerful an incentive as a gunpoint.

So when James opens his door to the peacekeepers, the first thing he sees is the love and respect in their eyes. He doesn't want to lose that, so he invites them into his kitchen to hold his shame with him. In this world, shame and guilt aren't things we hold alone anymore. James learned in grade school that these are things we hold and resolve in community.

"What happened?" one peacekeeper asks.

James speaks. The peacekeepers hear a story about a co-dependent relationship darkened by emotional abuse, and about Pelia breaking the cycle by leaving. James felt angry, powerless, and broken; and, acting on a perverted, fractured logic, he tried to put himself back together by hurting Pelia.

"I'm sorry, James," says his high school friend. He's not apologizing to absolve James of accountability. Everyone in the room knows that James will be held accountable. He apologizes because he and James used to see each other twice a month, but the peacekeeper's responsibilities as a new father meant he and James hadn't been in regular contact. "I had no idea you were struggling this hard."

"I'm sorry," says another peacekeeper, the one who'd been coming to know and like James at community events. "I didn't see you struggling this hard, but I did have some concerns about the way you talked about your relationship. I convinced myself that it wasn't a problem because . . . well, because I don't have an easy time making friends. And I was afraid I was being too judgy, that I might alienate you, and . . . lose the chance for you to get to know me."

The men cry, because in this new world, men weep when they hurt.

"I'm sorry, James," says the third peacekeeper. Before coming to James's house, the three peacekeepers had met to share knowledge, during which they learned that James had lost his mother the month before in a car accident. The two had had a complicated relationship, but the peacekeepers imagined that the painful loss of the two primary female figures in James's life had plunged him into a dark place.

"I'm sorry," James whispers. He's closing a ritual they all learned in grade school, the starting point on the path toward restoration when someone commits harm.

"Pack a bag," his high school friend says. "We'll send movers to take the rest of your things to storage until you've been reborn back into the community."

The four pile into a sedan, two peacekeepers in the back, James in the passenger seat. While they drive, the peacekeepers in the backseat sing ritual songs in low tones of remorse, death, and future rebirth. James occasionally joins in to strengthen the sounds that shake the grief and fear from his bones. They ascend into the mountains two hours outside the city, and they close their ritual songs with silence. They park beneath the trail that leads to a Healing City called Olo.

"The trail is another two hours," a peacekeeper says to James. "Can you walk?"

James feels tired from the ritual singing. "Can we drive?"

The four sit in silence before another peacekeeper speaks. "There are several ways up for people who can't walk a long distance. But the walk is important. It's part of the journey."

The four sit in silence again. After a few minutes, the driver toggles the windows down. They sit.

"I'm ready to walk," James says. They walk. They arrive at Olo, where the town's caretakers greet him with fierce hugs and a short welcome song. Anyone within earshot stops what they're doing and adds their voice. The peacekeepers say loving goodbyes. Each of them knows something admirable about James, and before they part, they remind him of these parts of himself. James cries again.

James spends his first three days in orientation circles, learning the oral histories, traditions, and rules of Olo. He settles in a large tent with two other people in their own process of rebirth. He spends the next year in restorative justice circles and one-on-one sessions coming to terms with the harm he's done, developing the personal skills to repair it, and learning about the shifts he needs to make in his imagination before his rebirth ceremony.[2] At the end of the year, he integrates his growth with a five-day vision quest in the wilderness outside Olo. He returns to a celebratory festival for him and the other people returning from their vision quests. They eat and dance and laugh themselves to exhaustion.

James spends his next year living in community. He enjoys a job cooking and tending fire for a collective of cannabis farmers. He learns to facilitate restorative justice circles for new guests on their rebirth journey. He sometimes teaches bookkeeping, a skill he brings from his former life. He doesn't begin a new romantic relationship, but not because it's against the rules. He's honoring a request. Pelia's restorative justice representatives have been receiving regular video reports from James about his growth, and in one of these reports James mentioned that he's beginning to trust himself enough to love healthily. These representatives have talked to Pelia to assess how much of James's process she wants to influence, and Pelia requested that James refrain from romantic relationships until after his rebirth ceremony. James yearns for partnership, but he honors Pelia's request.

One month into James's year living in community, he comes home to find a man tending the fire outside James's tent. He introduces himself as Yuto Kim. He says that the town's elders asked him to take James on as a student of Shibari, a rope art that involves tying people up in complex patterns and positions.

James is confused. He's heard about Shibari, and he associates it with leather-clad men tying up and hanging naked women from ceiling beams. Not only was James practicing abstinence, he'd come to Olo because he'd committed sexual harm; why would the elders disrupt his journey with BDSM? He voices his concern.

"Have you done Shibari before?" Yuto asks.

James shakes his head.

"Good," Yuto says. "Shibari can be sexual; it would be hard to do something different if that were already your practice. But the relationship between you, the rope, and your model does not need to be sexual. If you accept my offering, it will not be sexual. You will learn well how to exercise your power responsibly, with the proper consent of all involved. Including the rope itself. You will learn more about feeling powerless in service to something else."

James cries; he doesn't know why. The two sit and listen to the fire. Yuto silently apologizes on behalf of the cis male community, who failed to teach James how to use power responsibly.

James continues his journey. His friends and family from his old life come to see him when they can. They meet his friends and peers in the town; James gives them a tour through Olo, invites them to sit in the circles he holds, shares his new passion for Shibari. Sometimes James leaves Olo with his visitors and spends the weekend in their homes. Today, many would consider allowing such visits to be an unreasonable risk. What if James leaves and doesn't come back? But James has no compelling reason to escape. He's in a community process where the cultural norm is compassionate accountability. What would he gain by leaving?

In today's retributive justice–centered society, jails have programs where incarcerated people leave the jail to work in the free world.[3] Most people in these programs return to their jail after work. Those who don't come back have generally left because they want to see family or friends, because they feel they're being treated unfairly, or because they want more autonomy. In Olo, the town's caretakers respect James's autonomy; James feels he's been treated fairly, and the tools he's learned at Olo have deepened his relationships with friends and family. He has no reason to run away. But if he did, Olo would send peacekeepers to find James and bring him back. And when he returned, the town's caretakers would both implement preventive measures against James's future escape and assess and engage the reasons James left in the first place.

But James doesn't leave. His rebirth ceremony is in six months. He's prepared. He's spent the last twelve months in one-on-one sessions with his restorative justice representative learning how to be accountable to Pelia. He's learned how to repair the harm he's caused and how to avoid exacerbating that harm by placing extra emotional labor on Pelia. He's practiced in mock sessions with his representative, because healing the harm you've caused is a learned skill. James has become an expert. Pelia has been preparing with her representatives to receive James's amends. She's developed a community to support her spiritually and emotionally, and she's worked through the healing she needs within herself to have the capacity to receive a sincere apology.

When the day comes, peacekeepers drive Pelia and nine supporters selected by her to Olo. They meet James on a plateau above the town, with the entire town seated in a circle to observe the ceremony. In the middle of the circle, James sits at a table. Sitting behind him, Yuto, James's family, and his restorative justice representative hum a song. They stop when Pelia arrives. She sits opposite James, and her supporters stand behind her. A facilitator sits between them at the head of the table.

No single blueprint exists for these ceremonies; only the goals are consistently the same: closure for the person harmed, amends and rebirth for the person who harmed. Pelia wants to speak first. She's angry with James, and she tells him. She tells him how much he hurt her in their relationship before her rape, and how the trauma of her rape impacted her over the years. She wants to know why he did it. James tells her, making it clear that he committed a horrible violation that she didn't deserve. Pelia has read the reports of James's transformation since arriving in Olo. She wants to hear it from him, so he shares the work he's done on himself and the ways in which he lives and relates differently. When it's James's turn to lead the conversation, he apologizes to Pelia, her family, her friends, his family, and his community. Then, each of Pelia's and James's supporters who wish to say something speak.

The ceremony is almost over. Pelia must decide whether James's apology is in itself enough. For her, it isn't, so James's supporters remove the table, and James removes his clothes and stands alone in a circle. He's naked except for a helmet and a protective cup for his genitals. Surrounding him, Pelia's supporters hold sticks. Pelia can join them, but she has decided against that. She will watch.

A drumbeat starts, and they beat James. James screams, buckles to the ground, but they continue. James's supporters wail, "Please, enough," but they continue. Bones fracture. Everyone knows that healing rifts in a community sometimes requires broken bones. They continue until the drums stop. It's been three minutes. James's body is broken, but his spirit feels whole. Consciousness fades in and out: he's rebirthing. The town of Olo begins to sing and dance around his body. Someone removes James's helmet. Someone pauses their dance to gift a gentle kiss on his brow. Pelia kneels beside him. They're both crying. She doesn't have to forgive him—many survivors never do forgive the person who harmed them. Like broken bones, broken hearts also have a place in healing journeys. But Pelia forgives him for the sake of her own peace: no words, just a nod of her head at his beseeching gaze. Then she walks away.

James's supporters ease him onto a litter and carry him to the medical center. The celebrants follow behind and range ahead, showering James and his procession with flowers, encouragement, and other gifts of love. James will eventually recover from his broken bones. He's free to leave Olo and never return, but he decides to stay to take a full-time job as a trainer for circle keepers. He will help other people who've committed harm in their communities with their rebirths. Just as there are cycles of harm, there's a cycle of healing, of which James has become a part.

The power distribution at the beginning of this second story was the same as it was in the first. I assigned the state 4 points, the community wherein the harm occurred, 3 points; James and Pelia, 1.5 points each.

After James hurt Pelia: James, 2.5; Pelia, 0.5.

After Pelia went to the peacekeepers (who are ultimately funded by the state) and they provided her with the resources and space to heal: Pelia, 1.5; James, 2.5; the state, 3.

After peacekeepers detained James, denying him a measure of autonomy: Pelia, 1.5; James, 1; the state, 4.5.

After James's rebirth ceremony: Pelia, 2, both because she has grown and she has closure; for the same reasons, James also has 2. Because they grew in community, the stakeholder who lost resources is the community, so it is down from 3 to 2. Because the state partially supports the community, the delivery of resources brings the community back to 3 and drops the state to 3.5. James remains in Olo, dedicating his resources to the town's healing mission, bringing the community to 3.5. By the end of the cycle of harm between Pelia and James, power has been redistributed. The state has 3.5 points; the community, 3.5; James, 1.5; Pelia, 2.

Compare this to the outcomes from the first story about robbery; those outcomes will always make the state stronger while the community and James get weaker.

Which system will produce safer communities? Which system takes better care of survivors of harm? Which better reintegrates people who've committed harm back into society? The second system delivers outcomes that transform the harm committed into opportunities for stronger communities. That is abolition's goal. The prisons and the police departments we seek to dismantle are merely the symptoms of a sick society, the obstacles we see in the way of achieving a healed society where everybody thrives.

How do we get to this healed society described in the second story? To properly answer that question, it's worth examining the historical context: How did we become entrenched in the dysfunctional world in which we currently live? Mass incarceration is the manifestation of our sick society that I know the most about, and I use it here as a fractal connected to the larger project of white supremacy.

The story arguably starts in 1968, when President Nixon inflamed a drug crisis so that he could prosecute a war against African American communities and racially code the effort as a war on drugs. Nixon's strategy came to light in 1994 when journalist Dan Baum interviewed Nixon's domestic policy adviser, John Ehrlichman, about the politics of drug prohibition. Baum was shocked when Ehrlichman waved off Baum's questions as irrelevant. "You want to know what this was really about?" Ehrlichman asked.

> The Nixon campaign in 1968, and the Nixon White House after that, had two enemies: the antiwar left and black people. You understand what I'm saying? We knew we couldn't make it illegal to be either against the war or black, but by getting the public to associate the hippies with marijuana and blacks with heroin, and then criminalizing both heavily, we could disrupt those communities. We could arrest their leaders, raid their homes, break up their meetings, and vilify them night after night on

the evening news. Did we know we were lying about the drugs? Of course we did.[4]

Nixon's strategy belongs to a long line of government policies that use law and punishment to both maintain white control over Black bodies and build white-controlled economies on Black backs.[5] Corporate interests invariably back these strategies with both money and false narratives published by trusted media sources. The pattern is as old as plantation slavery. After slavery was abolished, Southern governments passed hundreds of bad-faith vagrancy laws to arrest Black people and force them to work on plantations as prison slave labor.[6] Southern newspapers published waves of articles in support of re-enslaving Black people through this new convict-leasing system. They cast Black people as lazy criminals who constituted a Southern moral and economic crisis that vagrancy laws remedied. One newspaper wrote that at least five hundred Black criminals plagued Memphis, and that proper enforcement of vagrancy laws would capture "one thousand of the civil rights vagabonds."[7] Another newspaper described the South's undeniable "curse" as the "fact" that "negroes" are unwilling "to earn an honest living by hard work."[8] In an article about the world cotton supply, the *Charleston Daily News* objected to a low-yield forecast that attributed its prediction in part to unwilling Black workers, who lack "the energy and enterprise of the white worker." The newspaper criticized the forecast because the prediction didn't recognize that the problem of unwilling Black workers was a temporary one that would be remedied by vagrancy laws.[9]

Ultimately, an examination of how we arrived at our current world is an examination of power dynamics. It can be helpful, then, to identify the historical stakeholders, because keeping them front of mind as we examine their roles generation after generation can reveal the white supremacist patterns, strategies, and ideologies that we have the power to change. At this point in the discussion, we have the U.S government in the South, the media, white communities, and Black communities.

The emancipation of Black labor destabilized the economic power of the South, so Southern governments legislated and enforced laws to re-enslave Black people, while the media legitimized the government's atrocities in the public imagination of white America. Officials in the Nixon administration saw Black people organizing for equality as a threat to white political power, so they manufactured and inflamed moral panic about drugs. In their narrative, they cast Black people as the predators and junkies, and under the cover of the racist fear that was generated, they waged political and economic war on Black communities to continue the U.S. legacy of colonizing Black power for white success.

Nixon's commitment to white supremacy was bolstered by the FBI, which in recent years had launched its Counterintelligence Program (COINTELPRO) to disrupt the Communist Party in the U.S. In 1967, under the cover of the public's anti-communist hysteria, the FBI expanded the mission of COINTELPRO to destroy Black liberation movements.[10] In testimony before the U.S. Senate, Assistant FBI Director William C. Sullivan described the program's tactics as no holds barred in a rough business, testifying that the FBI used the same tactics on the civil rights movement as it used against Soviet spies.[11] It bears saying twice: the U.S. government deployed the same tactics that caused the fall of the Soviet Union, an empire with trillions of dollars in resources, against Black communities fighting for civil rights.

The FBI destroyed Black movements all over the U.S., but nowhere has that been more apparent in my life than in California, where I witnessed the damage done myself. When I was in prison, I organized cellblocks to participate in the legislative process to support a more progressive criminal justice agenda. I remember one night returning to my cell high on endorphins. I felt powerful because I was a part of the change I wanted to see. I reflected on how different my life and community would have been if I'd had meaningful access as a teen to political frameworks of change.

For me and my peers on the street, not only did we have few healthy outlets to exercise power, but we were kids: we didn't have the emotional awareness to understand we felt powerless. Unacknowledged powerlessness built up in us until it exploded in transgressions like violence. Martin Luther King Jr. explained that "riots are the language of the unheard." At the root of the life of crime that I chose was a sense of powerlessness and isolation, and an introduction to political activism would have remedied both problems.[12]

A decade after my organizing in prison, Robert Saleem Holbrook, executive director of the Abolitionist Law Center, summed up the impact of COINTELPRO on California. Holbrook and I are the same age, and after an interview I conducted for a documentary on solitary confinement, we bonded over our shared life experiences. He's from the East Coast, and I shared with him my grief about having a lack of political education as a kid. We talked about music; I grew up listening to N.W.A because their anger felt like an honest reflection of my reality. The problem with N.W.A's brand and what made them complicated was that their honesty helped win my trust of them, but what they offered in their response to injustice was simply to succeed at capitalism by any means necessary. Plenty of hip-hop artists on the East Coast expressed rage, too, but they also took it beyond rage to political analysis. I told Holbrook that I wish I'd had that exposure when I was young. I admitted that I felt embarrassed that I'm from the founding place of the Black Panthers, Oakland, yet knew very little about them until I was in my twenties in prison.

"You didn't know about them when you were a kid because the state erased them," Holbrook said. He went on to explain how California had major heavy hitters in movement work, but the state wiped their political work off the public map and replaced it with caricatured narratives of Black rage. In this regard, the FBI succeeded in its objective, and when it finished destroying the sources of political power in Black communities, the CIA moved in to facilitate the destruction of the social fabric. Most Generation X Americans remember the crack epidemic in inner cities. What many people don't know is the CIA played a key role in the epidemic.

In the 1980s, the CIA backed the Contra rebels and waged a proxy war against Nicaragua's revolutionary Sandinista government. Elements of the Contra rebels funded this war with cocaine trafficking in the U.S. The CIA's own documents reveal the agency's knowledge about this, showing they were at least somewhat complicit. The public learned about it when *San Jose Mercury News* reporter Gary Webb published a twenty-thousand-word exposé series in 1996 linking the CIA's proxy war to the subsequent crack epidemic that had devastated California's most vulnerable African American neighborhoods.[13] Thanks to what CIA Directorate of Intelligence staffer Nicholas Dujmovic described as "a ground base of already productive relations with journalists," the largest newspapers in the country descended to discredit Webb. For example, the *Los Angeles Times* assigned seventeen reporters to pick apart Webb's story.[14] Big media, arguably a proxy for the CIA, destroyed Webb's career, and eight years later, he supposedly committed suicide by shooting himself twice in the head with a .38-caliber revolver. Twice. To summarize, Webb broke a damning story on an American agency of white supremacist spies and assassins. The media, whose role in white supremacy is well established in my mind, eviscerated him, he lost his career, and then he's found dead after somehow managing to shoot himself twice in the head.

Although Webb's story is the most sensational, it wasn't the first to document the government's complicity. Eleven years before Webb's exposé, the Associated Press's Robert Parry and Brian Barger reported on the Contras' drug trafficking in the U.S., and President Reagan's administration ran a covert campaign to discredit all reporting on Contras and drugs.[15] The story prompted a Senate investigation that concluded with the release of the first report acknowledging that the U.S. conducted covert operations in Nicaragua, Panama, Haiti, and the Bahamas with knowledge of and tolerance for drug smuggling under the guise of national security.[16] The revelation received little coverage in the media, perhaps because of Reagan's covert campaign to kill it, perhaps because the CIA had the "ground base of already productive relations with journalists" that would later destroy Webb.

The FBI destroyed Black movements and the political power of their communities, and then the CIA facilitated, if not built, a bridge from these vulnerable communities to Contra cocaine traffickers, which destroyed the social and economic structures of the impacted communities. There's no hard evidence that the CIA caused the crack epidemic, and that is not surprising given that the CIA is a billion-dollar counterintelligence agency. It's nearly impossible for a lone investigator to collect the necessary evidence to win an information war against such a power. Whether or not that hard evidence exists, the crack epidemic that may have never happened but for the actions and policies of the U.S. government fulfilled Nixon's faux prophecy of a drug crisis, which the U.S. government then used to wage war on Black communities.

Between Nixon's second year in office and the first story published about Contra cocaine trafficking in 1985, prison and jail populations nearly doubled.[17] Crime rates rose by about 12 percent.[18] This is relevant not because it tells us something accurate about crime—crime rates are notoriously bad at measuring crime—but because crime rates make good proxies for arrest data. Police increased their arrest rate by disproportionately targeting Black people. By 1990, Black people would comprise 12 percent of the general population but more than half of the prison population.[19] More arrests of Black people meant more stories pushed by corporate media with sinister mugshots reinforcing a public panic that politicians, building on Nixon's strategy, would exploit in election campaigns.

In the 1988 presidential election, George Bush Sr. eviscerated Michael Dukakis by painting him as soft on crime. At the time, all fifty state prison systems supported weekend furloughs, which enabled incarcerated people to go home over the weekend as a reward for good behavior. During a furlough, Willie (now William) Horton raped a white woman and stabbed her partner in Massachusetts, where Dukakis had been governor. Through an independent group, Bush campaign strategist Lee Atwater produced a commercial that would become known as one of the most racist ads in modern political history.[20] It featured a picture of Bush along with his tough-on-crime credentials and a picture of Dukakis along with his soft-on-crime liabilities. The commercial sensationalized Horton's offenses committed while on a furlough and ended with the tagline: "Weekend Prison Passes[,] Dukakis On Crime."[21] This ad became a central part of a presidential campaign that focused on a racialized fear of crime, and cemented tough-on-crime policy as the status quo in U.S. politics.[22] Worse, not only did the Nixons and Bushes of the world stoke delusions about the causes of rising crime, they did so, I believe, with knowledge that U.S. government projects like COINTELPRO were more responsible for rising crime than "lenient" criminal justice policies ever could be.

Two years after Bush's election in 1988, the Pentagon began the militarization of police forces. The Department of Defense used a program called "1033" to send surplus military equipment to law enforcement, ostensibly to combat the drug crisis that the U.S. government helped create.[23] "More funding for police" became every politician's talking point even when crime was falling. Police and their unions became big business with big influence and little accountability. By the twenty-first century, and despite a wave of progressive criminal justice reform bills, the U.S. was arresting and incarcerating at higher rates than any country in the world.[24] The vast majority of the people incarcerated were people of color.

The story of how we got here is essentially about the lengths white supremacists will go to preserve white power. It's about a government accountable not to its people but to preserving white supremacy for white citizens, and the most powerful representation of those white citizens are corporations. It's about corporate and police power vested in preserving this supremacy because their own power was built on it, and the central theme of the story is the misallocation of power.

How do we exit this story? How do we get to the healed society described in the second story? We do it by restructuring our society and balancing power so that government is accountable and in service to communities, and corporations are accountable to government. Today, government power is supposed to be checked in two ways: through the separation of its powers into the legislative, judicial, and executive branches, and through elections. This design has failed. Our two-party system renders the people's will irrelevant.[25] Politicians are loyal to their parties, who are ultimately controlled by corporate interests, not the public. When politicians violate public trust to serve their own interest within their party, voters can only replace them with another candidate who will continue the same business as usual. The separation of government powers has also failed because its design scheme misses the most powerful player: corporations.

Day 0 of the healed world in the second story begins when we create a system of balances and checks that not only accounts for the relevant power centers but also harnesses their power to support the life and growth of communities. We re-envision governance. We separate corporations from the executive, judicial, and legislative branches in the same spirit of separating church and state. We end corporate lobbying and campaign finance. We introduce a new arm of government called the "community branch," a local body of council members, executives, and magistrates responsible both for local governance and for setting the agenda for state representatives. Community control of state legislation would give us the land trusts that eventually evolve into Healing Cities. It would give us the peacekeepers. It would give us school curricula that teach James that we resolve shame and guilt in community.

These community branches would serve the foundation of a bottom-up government. Fifty percent of the body's members would be selected by a census board that appoints residents who've lived the longest in each district. Each district would elect another group composed of 30 percent of the community branch's members, and the remaining 20 percent of the body would be nominated by their neighbors in recognition of the major contributions to the communities in which they live.

These local bodies would also serve as a check on corporate power. While business interests wouldn't be permitted to lobby legislators or finance political candidates, they could petition for their interests to the community branch. Their currency in these situations wouldn't be money but a presentation, first, of how their request would benefit the communities within which they operate, and second, why the corporation's industry would need the proposed legislation in order to thrive. In this way, businesses would have the freedom to grow but not at the expense of the communities often impacted by their profit drives.

How do we get to a healed world where we don't need or want prisons? Where white supremacist government and money politics are dismantled, and community power arises in their wake? At the heart of this power would be citizen councils, executives, and magistrates—a democracy grown from the grassroots. A real democracy. We would commit to a path where we nurture growth, meet harm with accountability tempered by compassion, and justice becomes not just a verdict but an ongoing journey toward collective healing.

7

How to Change Anything

We can collectively transcend the imagination problem and change any social condition by combining two lessons I learned in prison. The first lesson is a version of radical orientation: start small, iterate on larger and larger scales, and these iterations will teach you how to change conditions. The strategy relies on a theory of fractals, described by adrienne maree brown, that conceives of complex systems as a series of simple, self-same patterns that repeat at different scales.[1] What Brown concluded after applying this theory for decades in social justice settings is that the patterns we create and repeat on a small scale become the same patterns that emerge on a large scale. Grace Lee Boggs describes the wisdom in Brown's conclusion another way: "Transform yourself to transform the world."

Transform the small to transform the big: that's the story of my life.

The first abolitionist project I developed focused on language. I'd encountered essays by Angela Davis in which she writes about why we must abolish prisons and how words like "inmate" and "convict" dehumanize incarcerated people.[2] As I read, I began to think through my experiences with the thousands of volunteers who came into San Quentin to support self-help programs. New volunteers find themselves shocked and transformed by the compassion, intelligence, and resilience they encounter in incarcerated people, but they have a hard time conveying those experiences in prisons to their friends and families. Often they must reduce their explanations to "You just have to come and see what I'm seeing." These volunteers struggle to communicate their experiences because it's something that's almost impossible to explain. That is because the narratives embedded in words like "prisoner" and "inmate" are incompatible with perceptions of them as compassionate, deserving, amazing human beings. In essence, when people try to convey the human value of a "prisoner," they are inadvertently expressing something other than respect for that individual and their human value. I was expressing something other than respect about myself and my peers each time I wrote the word "inmate" in my articles for the *San Quentin News*, and I wanted to change this practice.

I started small. I stopped using "inmate," "prisoner," "offender," and "convict." The change in my incarcerated community and in the field of media would of course take longer, but I proceeded with the next level up from my personhood: my personal relationships. I talked to my Prison Renaissance co-founders, Juan Meza and Rahsaan Thomas. Although we disagreed on what the alternative terms for "inmate" and "prisoner" should be, we still agreed to make a shift in the language we used. Rahsaan, also a journalist, and I changed the language in our bios and made the same shift in the articles we wrote. I would talk to the literary magazine editors who objected to the long syllable count of "Incarcerated-Americans," but the personal relationships we'd already developed allowed them to trust in and support my commitment to more responsible language. In the plays we performed for the public, Juan and I—performing artists ourselves—convinced some of our fellow artists to include liberal use of "incarcerated-American."[3] Juan and I shared close relationships with many of the volunteers who came into San Quentin State Prison, so they were more than happy to serve as ringers in the audience. In the question-and-answer session that followed each performance, volunteers would raise their hands and say something like, "I noticed you guys are saying 'Incarcerated-American' and not 'prisoner.' Why?" The ensuing conversations fueled a change that started gradually but gained momentum.[4]

The next level up from personal relationships was professional relationships. I brought my concerns about dehumanizing language to the next editorial meeting at the *San Quentin News*. The editors struggled to listen to me and expressed outrage: we were supposed to be journalists, not activists, and "inmate" was more concise than "Incarcerated American." Moreover, they argued that incarcerated people had "real problems"; they want fair sentences and more rehabilitative opportunities.

I persisted. The newsroom often hosted guests from both the worlds of journalism and advocacy. At every opportunity, I steered the conversation toward the imperative of changing the language we use for incarcerated people.[5] Bill Keller, former editor in chief of the Marshall Project, published an op-ed about one such conversation.[6] For Keller, there wasn't a clear consensus on usage, and he seemed to feel that as a journalist, he shouldn't choose a side. He believed embedded narratives lurked beneath words like "felon." As a leader in his field, he had the power to change the accepted standards of journalism. The Marshall Project would eventually adopt "incarcerated person" as standard usage. It would become a wider practice in media in general, extending all the way up to the Department of Justice, but at the time, Keller was no more willing to challenge the convention than *SQN*'s editors were.[7]

A story about federal judges and a friend of mine provides a lens to examine Keller's resistance to change. My friend, a defense attorney, met with judges to talk about sentencing reform and the ways that retributive justice is destroying the U.S. One judge shared an honest reflection. He told my friend that if they started giving lower sentences because retributive justice was out of hand, that would mean that for decades they'd been over-sentencing people. Beneath this statement lurks a hard question that these judges must come to terms with: *How do I live with myself? I swore to uphold justice, and I have been a willing instrument of injustice for decades.*

The first key to changing anything is building knowledge—that is, building the *potential* power to do. *SQN*, Keller, the judges, society in general—all of us have access to much of the knowledge we need to change social conditions. The second key to changing anything is building capacity—that is, building the *actual* power to do. As a society, we have a lot of knowledge but very little capacity, and I measure that lack of capacity by our propensity to turn away from ugly truths about the world and about ourselves.

I've always been the hero of my own story. I never hurt someone who hadn't hurt me first. That was the case until junior high school, when my friends challenged me to punch a Vietnamese boy for nothing. It was a game some Black kids played, a trauma-based reaction to the model minority myth that explicitly portrays Asians as innately law-abiding and intelligent while implicitly arguing that Black people are innately unruly and dumb.[8]

It started as a joke. Hassaan, Zeke, and I loitered outside a liquor store while our classmates streamed toward nearby bus stops. I was waiting there for a particular girl and they were acting as my wingmen. Zeke pointed at three Vietnamese kids crossing an overpass across the street. The first kid stared back, gripping the straps of his backpack like a parachutist about to jump off the curb. The other two were girls; they white-knuckled textbooks to their chests.

My friends and I mocked their fear in one breath and in the next condemned the boy for not being afraid enough.

"Who this nigga think he is?" Zeke said as he handed Hassaan the Hav-A-Tampa cigar we were smoking.

"Sir Lancelot," I said.

"I want to be *saaaaaaved*," Hassaan sang in a falsetto voice, mimicking the chorus of a rap song by E-40 that derided chivalrous men. Bobbing as if dancing to the track, he slowly pumped his fists, smoke trailing from the cigar vised between his knuckles. His hair fell in silken curls because his mother was white. Dancing on the corner, smiling with his eyes closed, he looked like a young Michael Jackson.

Malice simmered beneath our jokes. In our minds, the effeminacy of Asian men attached to the model minority myth, and hypermasculinity attached to our internalized myth of Black men. We felt outraged that he would stare us down like a man.

"E, you should sock that fool," Hassaan said.

Something whimpered in me. Fighting scared the shit out of me, but heroes weren't afraid. I'd grown up pretending I loved fighting.

"You fixin' to get E's ass kicked out here," Zeke said. Classic bait: it's a dog whistle for *you're not going to do it because you're afraid you'll get your ass kicked.*

I made myself laugh and turned to Hassaan. He was my best friend. "Nigga, pass the Tampa."

Hassaan withdrew the cigar from my reach and pointed the fingers holding it at Zeke. "E been to juvie; he ain't soft."

"Bitches go to jail all the time," Zeke said. "Dude's dad like a doctor or some shit."

Hassaan's temper showed around his mouth, lips pursing. Zeke wasn't just implying that I was soft. He was implying Hassaan was soft by association with me.

The crossing light switched from the red hand to the walking man. The Vietnamese kids began to cross the street, the boy gripping his straps, the girls clutching their books.

"E, sock that fool," Hassaan said, looking at Zeke.

I wasn't smiling anymore. By this time, I'd rejected my father and most of the principles for which he stood—honor your parents, get an education, work harder, save money, put God first. One principle had stuck: never throw the first punch; never start the fight. My father had been bullied as a kid, and from him, I learned to hate bullies.

"E . . ."

But heroes don't let their teams down.

"E!"

"Hey!" I skipped my foot off the curb and hopped onto the street. The Vietnamese boy averted his gaze and veered outside the crosswalk. I quickened my step and caught him. I wanted to punch him, to have it finished. I couldn't. I couldn't, and that frustrated me so much that I did something worse. I grabbed his backpack and wrestled with him until I tore it from his grip.

"Bounce!" I said, and he prodded the girls to run ahead of him before he followed. His backpack sagged from the strap I held. I flung it into the gutter, returned to the corner.

I was thirteen years old, the first time I'd robbed someone, but like the judges, Keller, and *SQN*'s editors, I turned away from what I was doing. I would be in my twenties before I acknowledged that I had robbed him, but that day in junior high school, I was a hero. I'd maintained my integrity: don't be afraid, don't disappoint your friends, never throw a punch unless someone punches you first.

But I wasn't a hero. I was a bully. I hated bullies, which meant I hated myself, and I turned away from that as well to continue loving myself.

When I was sixteen, I hurt someone who hadn't hurt me first again. I'd paroled from the California Youth Authority carrying the scares of multiple stints in solitary confinement. My father had given up trying to guide me. He couldn't guide me because he'd overly relied on fear and violence to compel obedience, and after years of weightlifting and fighting in juvenile correctional institutions, I was a Black Hulk whose rage made him impervious to compulsion. I went from juvenile prison, to home, back to the street with my brothers in one week.

My oldest brother, Eddie, had become the king of the block during my time away. Timi and I both were crowned princes, but to the hood, I was Eddie's heir, the future, the hero. Fast forward to me playing enforcer in the back seat of Eddie's Oldsmobile Cutlass as he patrolled the neighborhood looking for the sex worker who owed him money for crack. The same fearful sadness from junior high wormed in my chest at the specter of violence, but it had grown tiny and distant over the years.

The name of the woman we hunted was Chaka—like Chaka Khan—the closest thing to an aunt I had. All of the sex workers in my neighborhood were aunts. They'd raised me, housed me, fucked me, and nurtured the hypermasculinity they believed I would need to survive street life. We finally found her working outside the neighborhood on East Fourteenth Street. I slipped out the car to approach her on the sidewalk while Eddie pulled up next to her.

"Where's my money, Chaka?"

She looked at him, turned around to spot me, screamed, and ran. She couldn't outrun me, so she darted into traffic. A smart move: I could beat her in the middle of the busiest street in East Oakland only for so long. I grabbed her hair, spun her around, and punched her.

She hit the ground covering her face. "I'm sorry, please!" Her terror washed over me.

My earliest memory was one of terror: my father beating my mother on the living room carpet. She screams like Chaka screams, as three-year-old me shrinks in the kitchen doorway, watching. Somehow, I find myself standing next to my mother. She's so terrified for her life that she grabs me, crushes me against the bones in her chest. I'm a human shield. Her motherly instincts go haywire. One moment she uses me as a shield; in the next, she's smothering me against the carpet protecting me with her back. I leave my body. I feel like I'm dying, but I don't know that feeling because three-year-olds don't yet know that death exists. My father snatches my arm. My joints nearly snap in their tug-of-war, and he tears me from her grip. My feet hit the ground running to the kitchen. I'll be running from that living room for the rest of my childhood. I'll love and hate my father for the rest of my life. I'll never be like him, never be an abuser who terrorizes women.

"I'm sorry, please!" Chaka crumpled to the ground. In my mind, I wasn't an abuser. This was business. Chaka knew the rules, she'd been one of the people who taught me the rules: meet your obligations, enforce your debts. She didn't meet her obligation, and it was my job to enforce the debt. I didn't like the rules, didn't make the rules; it was just the way the world worked. I hit Chaka again. Kicked her. Dragged her across the asphalt. Then I turned away.

The judges in my friend's story couldn't stop giving out excessive sentences because they couldn't face their complicity in a racist legal system. Keller and *SQN*'s editors resisted taking a stand against dehumanizing language because they struggled to face their complicity in a racist media institution. When I encountered Angela Davis's admonition against dehumanizing language, I heard it, faced it, and changed not just because I had the knowledge to change but because I'd spent decades building capacity to change. I built that capacity through the repeated practice of facing ugly truths. That capacity reached a tipping point when I finally faced that I had murdered a man.

The act of shooting someone made me emotionally numb. I was in the grief stage of denial for years, but gradually I came to accept it. It started with my daughter's birth. Not only did I begin to see the world through their eyes, my first major act of empathy as an adult, but I began to think about the world through the eyes of my victim's children. I'd taken their father. Just this fraction of the harm I caused felt world-ending. Although I acknowledged it, I didn't let the rest in; still, it was a crack in my dammed-up emotions that would inevitably widen.

I blocked feeling for the rest of his family. His sister hated me. I told myself she lied to herself because she knew the life my victim and I lived, knew that the day I murdered him he was already mobilizing his resources to kill me. But the more I sat in the agony of what I'd done to my victim's children, the less sense my resentment for his sister made. Of course, she hated me. I'd shot her brother. The stress of it would eventually contribute to her father's heart attack. The crack in my dam widened.

Years later, I lived in a cell with my oldest brother in High Desert State Prison. I was processing the harm I'd done. I'll call my victim Vince Payne, but that's not his name. I felt horrible for Vince's family, but I clung to the belief that he deserved my violence. The newspaper had said that I had killed Vince over an argument in a five-dollar dice game, and that sounded senseless to me. My ego believed I would never kill someone over five dollars. I killed him because he and I had been in a cold war for leadership of our neighborhood, and I held him responsible for members of his faction who'd shot both my brothers. When I shared my justifications with my brother, he looked confused. He asked me to say it again. And then he told me I was confusing Vince Payne with

Vince Brown. Payne, my brother told me, had nothing to do with him being shot.

"What?" I said.

I had killed a man for nothing. The crack in my emotional dam exploded. Every feeling I'd denied (shame, disillusionment, grief) flooded in with so much pressure that the trauma pushed me out of my body. I watched the scene from above: my brother staring blankly at the corporal me; the cell, a six-by-twelve-foot box with a toilet and bunk bed, the ceiling just under nine feet; me hovering somehow beneath that ceiling and yet so much farther away than nine feet, floating somewhere dark, transfixed by two brothers held in the droning orange light of a prison cell.

The four hardest moments in my life were killing Vince, realizing how my incarceration would hurt my daughter, receiving that letter from that kid in Solano State Prison who idolized me for killing Vince, and this moment when I had to face the grief of taking life, without rationalizations, denials, and justifications. I remember, when I raised my gun, the knowing on Vince's face, something in me screaming for me to stop. I betrayed myself, I pulled the trigger, and a part of me disappeared until that conversation with my brother. That was the part that pushed me out of my body when the dam broke. It was still screaming like a bone-white ghost that only I could hear, and all I could feel, as I hovered in and outside of that cell, was that I could not go back to that body. I would not survive.

This is when I learned how to change anything. There's a power that, when radically oriented toward a goal, can change everything. It requires surrendering that human instinct to protect the self at all costs and submitting to a faith that beyond that gate of self-protection lies a transcendent road. That kind of surrender requires powerful incentive. For me, it was the ego-killing love a father has for his children. My father had reached for that love, and though his hand had fallen short, his reaching had shown me the way.

My brother was staring at the corporal me, a muscular Black man, but the heart of that man was a child screaming from the pain of the murder I'd committed with his hands. A child still running to the kitchen as his mother screamed, still whimpering on a street corner as I forced him to rob a Vietnamese boy, still grieving in my brother's Oldsmobile as that young me became the worst part of my father. The child me. He would not survive without me. I came back. I came back and discovered the transcendent road that is grief.

Grief is a journey. I'd always thought I'd known this truth because I'd read about the five stages of grief from the seminal book *On Death and Dying*, but there's knowledge that lives in our heads, pads our sense of mastery in an unpredictable, scary world, and there's knowledge rooted in our physical body that can transform the world.[9] It's a journey I had often started but never finished, because the pain turned me toward the refuges of rationalization, denial, and my favorite self-protector, outrage. Over time, grief became just that: pain. But pain is just part of the journey. Beyond that pain is a power I can attest to but can't describe. Our hegemonic culture doesn't have the language to describe it; if we had the language to transmit an understanding of this power throughout our collective consciousness, white hegemony would crumble. It's a power that involves clarity of purpose and clarity about obstacles. It's a power that breaks the paralysis of helplessness. It's the answer to so many questions people ask me over and over. How did you write your way out of prison? How did you change your life? How do you keep transforming the world around you? How do you build powerful communities? That's incredible—how did you do that, know that, learn that? How are you so joyful, so kind, after all the trauma you survived?

The answer to all these questions is grief.

Acknowledgments

Thank you, ancestors, for planting the seeds that have guided, protected, and shown me all my life, culminating in the wisdom that grew this book.

Thank you to the men in prison who raised and saved me.

Thank you to my chosen families: you sustain me.

Thank you, Nayomi Munaweera, my love, my family, and the brilliant writer who helped me transform the chapter I hated into the most powerful thing I've written.

Thank you, James Forman Jr., for your stories that have shaped my hope for a just future. Thank you for your belief that I have something important to say and generously sharing my writing with the people who needed to see it.

Thank you, Camille Griep, Wendy Sawyer, Stephen Parrish, and Joni Labaqui, for the critical roles you played in my writer's journey. Thank you, Camille, for being my sister.

Thank you, David McCormick, my agent, for carrying my dream into reality.

Thank you, Mila Steele, for getting me off my ass to write this book.

Thank you to my editor, zakia henderson-brown, and The New Press. There's no such thing as great writers—only good writers and good editors who together make great works.

Notes

Introduction

1 See Christina J. Cross, Paula Fomby, and Bethany Letiecq, "Interlinking Structural Racism and Heteropatriarchy: Rethinking Family Structure's Effects on Child Outcomes in a Racialized, Unequal Society," *Journal of Family Theory & Review*, 14, no. 3 (2022): 482–501. https://doi.org/10 .1111/jftr.12458. Also see Andrea Smith, "Heteropatriarchy and the Three Pillars of White Supremacy: Rethinking Women of Color Organizing," in *Color of Violence: The INCITE! Anthology*, ed. INCITE! Women of Color Against Violence (Durham, NC: Duke University Press, 2016), 71–73.

2 Smith writes: "Patriarchy rests on a gender binary system in which only two genders exist, one dominating the other. Consequently . . . the colonial world order depends on heteronormativity. Just as the patriarchs rule the family, the elites of the nation-state rule their citizens." Smith, "Heteropatriarchy and the Three Pillars of White Supremacy," 72.

3 *I Am Not Your Negro*, directed by Raoul Peck (2016; Velvet Film, Artemis Productions, and Close Up Films).

4 Shadeed Wallace-Stepter, "Inside San Quentin: Moonlight," March 6, 2018, *Life of the Law* (podcast), produced by Shadeed Wallace-Stepter, https://www.lifeofthelaw.org/2018/03/inside-san-quentin-moon light.

5 See Nicki Lisa Cole, PhD, "What Is Cultural Hegemony?," ThoughtCo., January 6, 2020, https://www.thoughtco.com/cultural -hegemony-3026121.

6 Kivel writes: "Despite usually intense resistance, over time the worldview of the conquerors is internalized. It becomes accepted as natural and inevitable even by those dominated, although it is not in their best interests. One might say hegemony is 'the language of

conquest.'" Paul Kivel, *Living in the Shadow of the Cross: Understanding and Resisting the Power and Privilege of Christian Hegemony* (Gabriola Island, Canada: New Society Publishers, 2013), 2.

7 Gerbner writes: "Terms such as 'white' grew out of religious categories like 'Christian.'" Katharine Gerbner, *Christian Slavery: Conversion and Race in the Protestant Atlantic World* (Philadelphia: University of Pennsylvania Press, 2018), 12.

8 Aisha M. Jesús and Jemima Pierre, "Introduction to Special Section: Anthropology of White Supremacy," *American Anthropologist* 122, no. 1 (2020): 65–75, http://dx.doi.org/10.1111/aman.13351. Jesús and Pierre write, "[White supremacy as a global power system] emerged in the fifteenth century through the European expansion across the world" (67). See also Howard Winant, *The World Is a Ghetto: Race and Democracy Since World War II* (New York: Basic Books, 2001), 22–30.

9 Gerbner, *Christian Slavery*, 12, 26, 84, 89, 120, 131, 153, 179.

10 Gerbner writes, "Scholars have long recognized that whiteness emerged from the protoethnic term 'Christian.'" Ibid., 74.

11 See Magda Teter, *Christian Supremacy: Reckoning with the Roots of Antisemitism and Racism* (Princeton, NJ: Princeton University Press, 2023). Gerbner writes: "Protestant Supremacy was the predecessor of White Supremacy." Gerbner, *Christian Slavery*, 2.

12 Teter, *Christian Supremacy*, 3.

13 See David M. Goldenberg, *The Curse of Ham: Race and Slavery in Early Judaism, Christianity, and Islam* (Princeton, NJ: Princeton University Press, 2003). See also Charles Rivers, *The East African Slave Trade: The History and Legacy of the Arab Slave Trade and the Indian Ocean Slave Trade* (CreateSpace Independent Publishing Platform, 2017).

14 Winant writes: "To the extent that . . . [racialized modernity] deployed cultural instrumentalities—of interpretation, of representation,

of identification that made use of racial discourse—modernity was a culturally based racial project as much as it was an economically or politically based one." Winant, *The World Is a Ghetto*, 30.

15 Oliver Burkeman. "This Column Will Change Your Life: Near Enemies." *The Guardian*, June 19, 2018.

1. Rehabilitation, the Near Enemy of Personal Transformation

1 See Mark Duggan and S. Hertel, *The Politics of Correctional Labor: Unionization, Collective Bargaining, and Political Activity*, Brookings Institution, 2019. Also see Bruce Western and Becky Pettit, *Correctional Labor Unions and the Politics of Mass Incarceration*, National Institute of Justice, 2020.

2 See Traci Westmoreland, *Suitability Hearing Summary 1978–2022*, Board of Parole Hearings, December 22, 2023, https://www.cdcr.ca.gov /bph/2020/01/09/suitability-hearing-summary-cy-1978-through-cy-2018.

3 See Nazgol Ghandnoosh, PhD, Celese Barry, and Luke Trinka, *One in Five: Racial Disparity in Imprisonment—Causes and Remedies*, The Sentencing Project, January 16, 2024, https://www.sentencingproject .org/publications/one-in-five-racial-disparity-in-imprisonment-causes -and-remedies.

4 See "Race and Sentencing," National Association of Criminal Defense Lawyers, https://www.nacdl.org/Content/Race-and-Sentencing.

5 See Beth M. Huebner and Timothy S. Bynum, "Role of Race and Ethnicity in Parole Decisions," *Criminology* 46, no. 4 (2008): 907–38, https://www.ojp.gov/ncjrs/virtual-library/abstracts/role-race-and-ethnicity -parole-decisions; see also Sarah Mizes-Tan, "New Report Says California's Parole Process Could Lead to Inequitable Outcomes," CapRadio, January 13, 2023, https://www.capradio.org/articles/2023/01/13/new-report -says-californias-parole-process-could-lead-to-inequitable-outcomes.

6 For discussion on the discretion of police and prosecutors and structural racism, see Angela J. Davis, "Prosecution and Race: The Power and Privilege of Discretion," *Fordham Law Review* 67, no. 1 (1998), https://digitalcommons.wcl.american.edu/facsch_lawrev/1400; and Judge Juan Villaseñor and Laurel Quinto, "Judges on Race: The Power of Discretion in Criminal Justice," Law360, January 10, 2021, https://www.law360.com/articles/1330865/judges-on-race-the-power-of-discretion-in-criminal-justice. For the correlation between judicial discretion and racial disparities in sentencing, see Shawn D. Bushway and Anne Morrison Piehl, "Judging Judicial Discretion: Legal Factors and Racial Discrimination in Sentencing," *Law & Society Review* 35, no. 4 (2001): 733–64, https://doi.org/10.2307/3185415.

7 See California Code Regs., Title. 15; section 2402, subdivision (c): "Circumstances tending to show unsuitability [for parole] include: (1) the prisoner [committed] the offense in an especially heinous, atrocious or cruel manner, (2) previous record of violence, (3) unstable social history, (4) sadistic sexual offenses, (5) psychological factors, and (6) the prisoner [engaged] in serious misconduct in prison or jail."

8 *In re Lawrence* (2008) 44 Cal.4th 1181, 1214. The opinion also states, "A prisoner's lack of insight into his or criminal behavior or failure to take responsibility may provide the required nexus between the commitment offense and the prisoner's current dangerousness" (1228); and "the aggravated nature of the crime does not in and of itself provide some evidence of current dangerousness to the public unless the record also establishes that something in the prisoner's pre- or post-incarceration history, or his . . . current demeanor and mental state, indicates that the implications regarding the prisoner's dangerousness that derive from his . . . commission of the commitment offense remain probative to the statutory determination of a continuing threat to public safety" (1214).

9 See Kevin Sawyer, "Criminals and Gangmembers Anonymous Graduation," *San Quentin News*, January 18, 2018, https://sanquentin news.com/gangmembers-anonymous-graduation.

10 See Stokely Carmichael and Charles V. Hamilton, *Black Power: The Politics of Liberation in America* (New York: Random House, 1967). 124–27.

11 See Michael Stolp-Smith, "New Orleans Massacre (1866)," BlackPast.org, January 25, 2023, https://www.blackpast.org/african -american-history/new-orleans-massacre-1866; and Matt Mullen, "The New Orleans Massacre," *HISTORY*, July 25, 2023, https://www.history .com/this-day-in-history/new-orleans-massacre.

12 See Michael Stolp-Smith, "The Colfax Massacre (1873)," Black-Past.org, February 7, 2023, https://www.blackpast.org/african-american -history/colfax-massacre-1873; and Missy Sullivan, "The Colfax Massa-cre," *HISTORY*, April 13, 2023, https://www.history.com/this-day-in -history/colfax-massacre-louisiana.

13 See "1898 Wilmington Coup," n.d., North Carolina Depart-ment of Natural and Cultural Resources, https://www.dncr.nc.gov/1898 -wilmington-coup; and Daniel R. Biddle, "The Wilmington Massacre of 1898," Equal Justice Initiative, November 10, 2023, https://eji.org /news/wilmington-massacre-of-1898.

14 See History.com editors, "Rosewood Massacre—Overview, Facts & Legacy," *HISTORY*, January 10, 2023, https://www.history .com/topics/early-20th-century-us/rosewood-massacre; and "Jan. 5, 1923: White Mob Destroys Black Community of Rosewood, Florida," Equal Justice Initiative, https://calendar.eji.org/racial-injustice/jan/05.

15 See NowThis Impact, "COINTELPRO: Why Did the FBI Tar-get Black Activists Fighting for Equality? | NowThis," YouTube video, July 6, 2018, https://www.youtube.com/watch?v=cmuqmP50mRc. See also Virgie Hoban, "'Discredit, Disrupt, and Destroy': FBI Records Acquired by the Library Reveal Violent Surveillance of Black Leaders, Civil Rights Organizations," UC Berkeley Library, January 18, 2021, https://www.lib.berkeley.edu/about/news/fbi.

16 See Scot Brown, "The Politics of Culture: The US Organization and the Quest for Black 'Unity,'" in *Freedom North: Black Freedom Struggles Outside the South, 1940–1980*, ed. Jeanne F. Theoharis and Komozi Woodward (New York: Palgrave Macmillan, 2003), https://doi.org/10.1007/978-1-4039-8250-6_10.

17 See Official Kwanzaa Website, n.d., https://www.officialkwanzaawebsite.org/.

18 See "History of California Minimum Wage," n.d., California Department of Industrial Relations, https://www.dir.ca.gov/iwc/minimumwagehistory.htm.

19 See Frantz Fanon, *Black Skin White Masks* (New York: Grove Press, 2008), 201.

20 Ruth Wilson Gilmore writes, "A prison is a city that weighs heavily on the place where it is." Gilmore, "Forgotten Places and the Seeds of Grassroots Planning," in *Engaging Contradictions: Theory, Politics, and Methods of Activist Scholarship*, ed. Charles R. Hale (Berkeley: University of California Press, 2008), 44, https://escholarship.org/content/qt7z63n6xr/qt7z63n6xr_noSplash_9021ecc05a6334f2a7cadd94b96bd68e.pdf.

21 See U.S. Department of Justice, Census of State and Federal Correctional Facilities, 2005, Appendix Table 16, which reports that 775,469 incarcerated people participate in one or more work programs.

22 See U.S. Department of Justice, Census of State and Federal Correctional Facilities, 2005, Table 4, which reports that 295,261 correctional officers work at state and federal facilities.

2. Imagination Solutions

1 See Scott Shafer, "In California, Life with Parole Increasingly Leads to Freedom," NPR, May 26, 2014, https://www.npr.org/2014/05

/26/315259623/in-california-life-with-parole-increasingly-leads-to
-freedom.

2 "Appeal Court Decision Help," Superior Court of California, County of Kern, n.d., https://www.kern.courts.ca.gov/self-help/appeal -court-decision-help#:~:text=Appealing%20Court%20Decision,in%20 reversing%20the%20original%20ruling.

3 Jim Crow still lives on in California prisons. People are punished for expressions of interracial intimacy (e.g., playing games together, sharing a meal, living in the same cell).

3. The Lie of Personal Accountability

1 Ezra David Romero, "For These Black Bayview-Hunters Point Residents, Reparations Include Safeguarding Against Rising, Toxic Contamination," KQED, January 10, 2024, https://www.kqed.org/science /1979614/for-these-black-bayview-hunters-point-residents-reparations -include-safeguarding-against-rising-toxic-contamination. Also see Karpani Burns, "The Quick, Dangerous, Dirty Development of the Hunters Point Shipyard." *San Francisco Bay View*, October 7, 2022, https:// sfbayview.com/2022/10/the-quick-dangerous-dirty-development-of-the -hunters-point-shipyard.

2 Evan Sernoffsky, "6 Wounded as Gun Violence Escalates in SF's Bayview," KTVU FOX 2, February 16, 2021, https://www.ktvu.com/news /6-wounded-as-gun-violence-escalates-in-sfs-bayview.

3 Ibid. The city supervisor called for more police foot patrols because "people don't shoot people when there's police presence." Despite a recent increase of police officers in the area, the president of the San Francisco Police Officers Association was "concerned the department is operating with too few officers amid recent budget tightening." See also Andrew Sheeler, "Republican Lawmaker Calls for Armed Police Officers in Every California School," *Sacramento Bee*, February 21, 2024, https://www.sacbee .com/news/politics-government/capitol-alert/article285688511.html. In

response to public fear about school shootings, the conservative assembly-man covered in this article argued for mandating police in every school despite research showing that police not only fail to make schools safer but also make schools more dangerous for youth of color.

4 Ashitha Nagesh, "What Exactly Is a 'Karen' and Where Did the Meme Come From?," BBC, July 30, 2020. https://www.bbc.com/news/world-53588201.

5 For discussion of the war on drugs, see Dan Baum, "Legalize It All," *Harper's Magazine*, March 31, 2016, https://harpers.org/archive/2016/04/legalize-it-all.

6 In chapter four, "A Fight to Build Power," I talk about one key structural shift: changing the way nonprofit organizations support incarcerated people.

7 J.B.S. Haldane, "On Being the Right Size," *Harper's Magazine* 152 (1926): 424–27; see also Bryan L. Foster and Jelle Atema, "Crabs Do Not Pull Each Other Down: Experimental Evidence," *Animal Behaviour* 69, no. 5 (2005): 1097–99; and Lynne U. Sneddon and G. Byatt, "Cooperative and Competitive Crab Behaviour: Evidence from Experiments Using Barrels with Different-Sized Openings," *Animal Behaviour* 72, no. 3 (2006): 555–62.

4. A Fight to Build Power

1 "Shakespeare for Social Justice—the Power of Theatre," Marin Shakespeare Company, n.d., https://www.marinshakespeare.org/shakespeare-for-social-justice.

2 The concept of "zero-sum" comes from a branch of mathematics called game theory. For more on the concept, see Elliott Mendelson, *Introducing Game Theory and Its Applications* (New York: Chapman & Hall, 2004).

3   Madeleine Carlisle, "The Bail-Reform Tool That Activists Want Abolished," *The Atlantic*, September 2018, https://www.theatlantic.com /politics/archive/2018/09/the-bail-reform-tool-that-activists-want -abolished/570913.

4   The prison system started with 4 points; the philanthropic community, 3; Marin Shakespeare, 2; and incarcerated people, 1. After the intervention, the prison system has 5 points; the philanthropic community, 2; Marin Shakespeare, 2; and incarcerated people, 1.

5   Brooke Shelby Biggs, "Solitary Confinement: A Brief History," *Mother Jones*, March 3, 2009, https://www.motherjones.com/politics /2009/03/solitary-confinement-brief-natural-history.

6   California Code Regulations, Tit. 15, § 3400, states: "Employees must not engage in undue familiarity with inmates, parolees, or the family and friends of inmates or parolees. Whenever there is reason for an employee to have personal contact or discussions with an inmate or parolee or the family and friends of inmates and parolees, the employee must maintain a helpful but professional attitude and demeanor. Employees must not discuss their personal affairs with any inmate or parolee."

7   To summarize, the prison system started with 4 points; the philanthropic community, 3; the general public, 1; Prison Renaissance, 1; and incarcerated people, 1. After the intervention, the prison system has 2 points; the philanthropic community, 2; the general public, 3; incarcerated people, 2; and Prison Renaissance, 1.

5. Police Identity Behind the Blue Wall

1   See Sanders.senate.gov. "The Bernie Sanders College for All Fact Sheet," n.d. https://www.sanders.senate.gov/wp-content/uploads/college-for -all-fact-sheet-2019.pdf; see also Melanie Hanson, "How Much Would Free College Cost? | 2023 Cost Analysis," Education Data Initiative, August 31, 2023. https://educationdata.org/how-much-would-free-college-cost.

2 Rob Moore, "What Would It Cost to End Homelessness in America?—Scioto Analysis," Scioto Analysis, January 16, 2024. https://www .sciotoanalysis.com/news/2024/1/16/what-would-it-cost-to-end-homelessness -in-america. Moore writes, "eliminating homelessness in the United States should cost somewhere from $11 billion to $30 billion per year."

3 Urban Institute, "Criminal Justice Expenditures: Police, Cor- rections, and Courts," n.d. https://www.urban.org/policy-centers/cross -center-initiatives/state-and-local-finance-initiative/state-and-local -backgrounders/criminal-justice-police-corrections-courts-expenditures. "In 2021, state and local governments spent $135 billion on police (4 percent of state and local direct general expenditures), $87 billion on corrections (2 percent), and $52 billion on courts (1 percent)." See also Michael M. McLaughlin, Carrie Pettus-Davis PhD, Derek Brown PhD, et al. "The Economic Burden of Incarceration in the United States." Flor- ida State University, 2016, https://ijrd.csw.fsu.edu/sites/g/files/upcbnu 1766/files/media/images/publication_pdfs/Economic_Burden_of _Incarceration_IJRD072016_0_0.pdf. "The $80 billion spent annually on corrections is frequently cited as the cost of incarceration, but . . . [e]ven if one were to exclude the cost of jail, the aggregate burden of incar- ceration would still exceed $500 billion annually."

4 Alec Karakatsanis, "Police Departments Spend Vast Sums of Money Creating 'Copaganda,'" *Jacobin*, July 20, 2022, https://jacobin .com/2022/07/copaganda-police-propaganda-public-relations-pr -communications.

5 Associated Press, "LA County Sheriff Says Deputy Punching Baby-Holding Mother in the Face Was 'Completely Unaccept- able,'" KBCD, July 13, 2023, https://www.kcbd.com/2023/07/13/la -county-sheriff-says-deputy-punching-baby-holding-mother-face-was -completely-unacceptable/.

6 Chloé Cooper Jones, "Ramsey Orta Filmed the Killing of Eric Garner, So the Police Punished Him," *The Verge*, March 13, 2019, https://www.theverge.com/2019/3/13/18253848/eric-garner-footage -ramsey-orta-police-brutality-killing-safety.

Notes

7 Ibid. Jones writes, "But Santana did not immediately release what he'd recorded. Having followed the Eric Garner case, Santana knew Orta had been incarcerated. He knew justice was rare and witnesses were in danger of police retaliation. . . . Santana has said in interviews that he held on to the video because he felt his life would be in danger."

8 Dakin Andone, "6 Ex-officers, Some of Whom Called Themselves 'the Goon Squad,' Plead Guilty to State Charges in Torture of 2 Black Men," CNN, August 14, 2023.

9 Aria Jones and Kelli Smith, "Fired Southlake Cop Posed with Swastika Texted to Citizen, Records Say," *Dallas News*, August 3, 2003.

10 Jonathan Macheca's profile, LinkedIn, accessed August 23, 2023, https://www.linkedin.com/in/jonathan-macheca-77a385282/.

11 For demographics of Southlake Police force, see "Become a Southlake Police Officer," City of Southlake (TX) official website, https://www.cityofsouthlake.com.

12 Cerise Castle, "How the Lynwood Vikings Paved the Way for LASD Gangs," *Knock LA*, February 27, 2023, https://knock-la.com/lynwood-vikings-sheriff-gang-origins-abuse/.

13 Steven Greenhouse, "How Police Unions Enable and Conceal Abuses of Power," *New Yorker*, June 18, 2020.

14 William P. Jones, *Police Collective Bargaining and Police Violence*, Community Change and Center for Labor and a Just Economy at Harvard Law School, September 2023, https://clje.law.harvard.edu/app/uploads/2024/04/9.17.23_Police-Collective-Bargaining-and-Police-Violence_FINAL.pdf. Jones writes, "The rise of police unions has generally correlated to an increase in police violence and decreased accountability for police." See also Dhammika Dharmapala, Richard H. McAdams, and John Rappaport, "Collective Bargaining Rights and Police Misconduct: Evidence from Florida," *Journal of Law, Economics, and Organization* 38,

205

no. 1 (March 2022): 1–41, https://doi.org/10.1093/jleo/ewaa025. The authors write: "Collective bargaining rights led to a substantial increase in violent incidents."

15 NAACP, "The Origins of Modern Day Policing," December 3, 2021, https://naacp.org/find-resources/history-explained/origins-modern-day-policing#:~:text=The%20origins%20of%20modern%2Dday,runaway%20slaves%20to%20their%20owners. See also Kristian Williams, "The Origins of American Policing," in *Our Enemies in Blue: Police and Power in America* (Oakland, CA: AK Press, 2015), 23–40.

16 Greenhouse, "How Police Unions Enable and Conceal Abuses of Power." For discussion of labor strikes and the relationship between capitalism and white supremacy, see Cedric J. Robinson, *Cedric J. Robinson: On Racial Capitalism, Black Internationalism, and Cultures of Resistance*, ed. H.L.T. Quan (London: Pluto Press, 2019).

17 Greenhouse, "How Police Unions Enable and Conceal Abuses of Power."

18 Srijita Datta, "Police Unions Spend Millions Lobbying to Retain Their Sway over Big US Cities and State Governments," *OpenSecrets News*, July 20, 2022, https://www.opensecrets.org/news/2022/06/police-unions-spend-millions-lobbying-to-retain-their-sway-over-big-us-cities-and-state-governments/.

19 Urban Institute. "Criminal Justice Expenditures: Police, Corrections, and Courts," n.d. https://www.urban.org/policy-centers/cross-center-initiatives/state-and-local-finance-initiative/state-and-local-backgrounders/criminal-justice-police-corrections-courts-expenditures. "In 2021, state and local governments spent $135 billion on police . . ."

20 Adam Elmahrek, "Police Reform Activists in Santa Ana Hit Union Backlash," *Los Angeles Times*, September 3, 2020, https://www.latimes.com/california/story/2020-09-03/defund-police-union-backlash-george-floyd-santa-ana.

21 Ibid.

22 See Reuven Blau, "Eric Adams' New Jail Commissioner Pushes Out Acclaimed Head of Investigations," *The City*, October 12, 2023, https://www.thecity.nyc/2022/01/04/eric-adams-jail-commissioner-pushes-out-acclaimed-investigations-head/. Also see Reuven Blau, "Adams' Ties to Lobbying Firm That Represents Jail Workers Raises Questions on Rikers Island Future," *The City*, November 1, 2021, https://www.thecity.nyc/2021/10/31/eric-adams-rikers-island-ties-to-correction-officer-lobbyist.

23 Kyle Brown, "Report Finds Minneapolis Was Wrongly Denied Federal Grant over 'Defund the Police' Rhetoric," KSTP, March 19, 2024, https://kstp.com/kstp-news/top-news/report-finds-minneapolis-was-wrongly-denied-federal-grant-over-defund-the-police-rhetoric/.

24 Ibid.

25 Ibid.

26 Carlos Granda, "'They Are a Cancer': Deputy Gangs Still Operating Within LA County Sheriff's Department, Report Says," ABC7 Los Angeles, March 4, 2023, https://abc7.com/los-angeles-county-sheriffs-department-deputy-gangs-report-2023-civilian-oversight-commission/12911222.

27 Hectar Tobar, "Deputies in 'Neo-Nazi' Gang, Judge Found: Sheriff's Department," *Los Angeles Times*, March 10, 2019, https://www.latimes.com/archives/la-xpm-1991-10-12-me-107-story.html.

28 Cerise Castle, "White Supremacist LASD Gang the Lynwood Vikings Terrorized Their Community," *Knock LA*, February 27, 2023, https://knock-la.com/lynwood-vikings-darren-thomas-class-action.

29 Frantz Fanon, *The Wretched of the Earth* (New York: Grove Press, 1968), 89–92.

30 Ibid.

31 David Lynn, "The Sheriff's Lynwood Gang," *Press-Telegram*, October 25, 1990, https://knock-la.com/wp-content/uploads/2021/03/The-Sheriffs-Lynwood-Gang.pdf.

32 Castle, "How the Lynwood Vikings Paved the Way for LASD Gangs."

33 Kenneth Reich and Edward J. Boyer, "Early Praise Gave Way to Criticism as Problems Grew in Department," *Los Angeles Times*, October 30, 1998, October 30. Block is quoted saying, "I would say that much of this has the smell, if you will, of a group of gang members in the community who, perhaps, are banding together and trying to discredit the deputies who work in this area."

34 James G. Kolts, *The Los Angeles County Sheriff's Department*, Civil Rights Litigation Clearing House, July 1992, p. 323, https://clearinghouse.net/doc/10910/.

35 Eric Lichtblau, "Block, Activists Spar over Abuse, Racism Charges," *Los Angeles Times*, September 14, 1996.

36 Reich and Boyer, "Early Praise Gave Way to Criticism as Problems Grew in Department."

37 Michael German, *Hidden in Plain Sight: Racism, White Supremacy, and Far-Right Militancy in Law Enforcement*, Brennan Center for Justice, August 2020, https://www.brennancenter.org/our-work/research-reports/hidden-plain-sight-racism-white-supremacy-and-far-right-militancy-law#footnote3_th6zsqx.

38 Ibid.

39 Ibid.

40 Ibid.

41 Ibid.

42 Bill Cummings and Jacqueline Rabe Thomas, "CT's Top Pros-ecutor to Investigate State Police False Ticket Scandal," *CT Insider*, June 30, 2023, https://www.ctinsider.com/news/article/ct-state-police -ticket-fraud-18177605.php.

43 Anne-Marie O'Connor and Tina Daunt, "The Secret Society Among Lawmen," *Los Angeles Times*, March 24, 1999, https://www .latimes.com/archives/la-xpm-1999-mar-24-mn-20461-story.html.

44 Ibid.

45 Sheriff Commission Oversight Commission, *Report and Recom-mendations of the Special Counsel to Sheriff Civilian Oversight Commission Regarding Deputy Gangs and Deputy Cliques in the Los Angeles County Sher-iff's Department*, County of Los Angeles, February 2023, p. 40, https://file .lacounty.gov/SDSInter/bos/commissionpublications/report/1138014_De putyGangsSpecialCounselReporttoCOC3.2.2023.PDF.PDF.

46 Alene Tchekmedyian, "Sheriff's Deputies Sue County, Accusing Banditos Colleagues of Beatings, Withholding Backup," *Los Angeles Times*, September 20, 2019.

47 Maggie Clancy, "A Thorough-But-by No-Means-Exhaustive List Explaining Why Sheriff Alex Villanueva Needs to Resign," *Knock LA*, February 1, 2022, https://knock-la.com/la-sheriff-alex-villanueva -must-resign-banditos-defund-police-e7019a6593df/.

48 Maya Lau and Matt Stiles, "Deputy Reinstated by Sheriff Vil-lanueva Admitted to Having Tattoo Linked to Secret Society," *Los Angeles Times*, March 29, 2019.

49 Joe Brizzolara and Kevin Flores, "After 7 Years of Cover-Ups, Surveillance, and Costly Police Killings, LBPD Critics Say Chief Luna Unfit to Be Sheriff," *Knock LA*, January 13, 2023, https://knock-la.com /lbpd-robert-luna-sheriff-campaign-lasd-long-beach/.

50 Ibid.

51 Ibid.

52 For example, see Danny Westneat, "'Feel Safer Yet?' Seattle Police Union's Contempt Keeps Showing Through," *Seattle Times*, September 16, 2023.

6. A Vision of Abolition

1 Before the intervention, the state had 4 points; the community had 3 points; James and Pelia had 1.5 points each. After the intervention, the state has 7 points; the community, 1; Pelia, 2; and James, 0.

2 Restorative Justice circles are community conversations where participants address harmful behavior and co-create a path toward accountability and community healing.

3 See "Work Release Program," Placer County, CA, 2008, https://www.placer.ca.gov/2008/Work-Release-Program#:~:text=The%20Work%20Release%20Program%20allows,in%20lieu%20of%20jail%20time.

4 Dan Baum, "Legalize It All," *Harper's Magazine*, March 31, 2016, https://harpers.org/archive/2016/04/legalize-it-all/.

5 Michelle Alexander, *The New Jim Crow: Mass Incarceration in the Age of Colorblindness* (New York: The New Press, 2010).

6 Douglas A. Blackmon, *Slavery by Another Name: The Reenslavement of Black Americans from the Civil War to World War II* (New York: Doubleday, 2008).

7 "Ledger Notes," *Public Ledger*, June 12, 1874, available at https://www.newspapers.com/image/227753571/?terms=vagrancy&match=1.

8 "It Won't Do," *Kansas State Record*, December 16, 1874, available at https://www.newspapers.com/image/366991654/?terms=%22vagrancy%20laws%22%20&match=1.

9 "The Cotton Supply," *Charleston Daily News*, November 23, 1865, available at https://www.newspapers.com/image/72079563/?terms=%22vagrancy%20laws%22%20&match=1.

10 Virgie Hoban, "'Discredit, Disrupt, and Destroy': FBI Records Acquired by the Library Reveal Violent Surveillance of Black Leaders, Civil Rights Organizations," UC Berkeley Library, January 18, 2021, https://www.lib.berkeley.edu/about/news/fbi. According to an FBI memo, the goal of COINTELPRO was to "expose, disrupt, misdirect, discredit, or otherwise neutralize" the radical fight for Black rights—and Black power.

11 Ibid.

12 It's not a surprise that I found political activism in prison, given that the U.S. government's number-one priority in the 1960s and '70s was to extract political leaders from Black communities and cage them and their knowledge in prisons.

13 Ryan Devereaux, "How the CIA Watched Over the Destruction of Gary Webb," *The Intercept*, July 21, 2015, https://theintercept.com/2014/09/25/managing-nightmare-cia-media-destruction-gary-webb/.

14 Ibid.

15 Peter Kornbluh, "Crack, the Contras, and the CIA: The Storm over 'Dark Alliance,'" *Columbia Journalism Review* 35, no. 5 (1997), https://nsarchive2.gwu.edu/NSAEBB/NSAEBB2/storm.htm.

16 Ibid.

17 "Data Toolbox," Prison Policy Initiative, n.d., https://www.prisonpolicy.org/data/. See specifically "State Prisons, Local Jails and Federal Prisons, Incarceration Rates and Counts, 1925–2022."

18 "United States Crime Rates 1960 to 2019," Disaster Center, n.d., https://www.disastercenter.com/crime/uscrime.htm.

19 Human Rights Watch. "United States—Punishment and Prejudice: Racial Disparities in the War on Drugs," 2000. https://www.hrw.org/reports/2000/usa/Rcedrg00-01.htm. "Between 1979 and 1990, the number of blacks as a percentage of all persons admitted to state and federal prisons increased from 39 to 53 percent." See also U.S. Census Bureau. "We, The American Blacks," Census.gov, October 8, 2021, https://www.census.gov/library/publications/1993/dec/we-01.html. "[The Black] population grew by 13 percent between 1980 and 1990, to about 12 percent of America's population."

20 Andrew Cohen, "George H. W. Bush, Grace, and Gracelessness," Brennan Center for Justice, December 3, 2018, https://www.brennancenter.org/our-work/analysis-opinion/george-h-w-bush-grace-and-gracelessness.

21 "The Campaign Ad That Reshaped Criminal Justice," *The Takeaway*, WNYC Studios, May 18, 2015, https://www.wnycstudios.org/podcasts/takeaway/segments/crime-reshaped-criminal-justice.

22 Ibid. For video, see llehman84, "Willie Horton 1988 Attack Ad," YouTube, November 4, 2008, https://www.youtube.com/watch?v=Io9KMSSEZ0Y.

23 Brian Miller, "The Militarization of America's Police: A Brief History," Foundation for Economic Education, May 24, 2019, https://fee.org/articles/the-militarization-of-americas-police-a-brief-history. See also Congressional Research Service, U.S. News and World Report, National Defense Authorization Act for Fiscal Year 1997, NPR, CBS, ACLU, Oxford University Press, NAACP-LDF and Texas Appleseed, ABC/Fusion, and DOD Excess Property. "1033 Program & Police Militarization," Report, March 23, 2018, https://www.fcnl.org/sites/default/files/documents/1033_and_police_militarization_fact_sheet_3_23_18.pdf.

24 "Incarceration Rates by Country 2023," World Population Review, n.d., https://worldpopulationreview.com/country-rankings/incarceration-rates-by-country.

25 Mehdi Alavi writes: "According to a 2022 Pew survey, only 32% of American adults feel that the two primary political parties adequately align with their views. That means that an overwhelming majority of Americans are not happy with the current government and election process." Mehdi Alavi, "The Colossal Corruption of the Two-Party System," *Fair Observer*, March 1, 2023, https://www.fairobserver.com/politics/the-colossal-corruption-of-the-two-party-system.

7. How to Change Anything

1 adrienne maree brown, *Emergent Strategy* (Edinburgh, Scotland: AK Press, 2017).

2 Angela Davis, *Are Prisons Obsolete?* (New York: Seven Stories Press, 2003).

3 We later abandoned this term because immigrants felt excluded by it.

4 We were not the only system-impacted people holding space for this dialogue. The Center for NuLeadership on Human Justice & Healing, a policy group of formerly incarcerated scholars and advocates, has been organizing around human-first language since 2006.

5 This was a very individualistic strategy on my part. It prioritized my goal of winning an argument rather than healing our community, but I still pushed forward, leaving them behind, both because I had a history of being hurt by them and because I knew I didn't need them to make the impact I wanted. If I could do it again, I would have taken a step down within the relational fractal and repaired my relationship with the *San Quentin News* editors, so that they could have greater trust in the importance and legitimacy of my proposal.

6 Bill Keller, "The Other F-Word," The Marshall Project, April 28, 2016, https://www.themarshallproject.org/2016/04/27/the -other-f-word.

7 National Institute of Justice, *National Institute of Justice Style Guide*, Department of Justice, 2022, p. 27, https://www.ojp.gov/pdffiles1 /nij/250404.pdf. The Department of Justice instituted a policy against using words like "inmate" to describe incarcerated people.

8 Kat Chow, "'Model Minority' Myth Again Used as a Racial Wedge Between Asians and Blacks," NPR, April 19, 2017, https://www .npr.org/sections/codeswitch/2017/04/19/524571669/model-minority -myth-again-used-as-a-racial-wedge-between-asians-and-blacks.

9 Elisabeth Kübler-Ross, *On Death and Dying* (New York, Macmillan, 1969).

About the Author

Emile Suotonye DeWeaver is a formerly incarcerated activist, widely published essayist, owner of Re:Frame LLC, and a 2022 Soros Justice Fellow. California's Governor Brown commuted his life sentence after twenty-one years for his community work. He has written for publications including the *San Francisco Chronicle*, the *San Jose Mercury News*, *Colorlines*, *The Appeal*, *The Rumpus*, and *Seventh Wave*. He lives in Oakland, California.

Publishing in the Public Interest

Thank you for reading this book published by The New Press; we hope you enjoyed it. New Press books and authors play a crucial role in sparking conversations about the key political and social issues of our day.

We hope that you will stay in touch with us. Here are a few ways to keep up to date with our books, events, and the issues we cover:

- Sign up at www.thenewpress.com/subscribe to receive updates on New Press authors and issues and to be notified about local events
- www.facebook.com/newpressbooks
- www.x.com/thenewpress
- www.instagram.com/thenewpress

Please consider buying New Press books not only for yourself, but also for friends and family and to donate to schools, libraries, community centers, prison libraries, and other organizations involved with the issues our authors write about.

The New Press is a 501(c)(3) nonprofit organization; if you wish to support our work with a tax-deductible gift please visit www.thenewpress.com/donate or use the QR code below.